FROM THE COLLECTION OF

GEORGE SCHNER, S.J.
1946 - 2000

IMAGINATION AND
INTERPRETATION IN
KANT

Rudolf A. Makkreel

IMAGINATION AND INTERPRETATION IN
KANT

The Hermeneutical Import of the
Critique of Judgment

The University of Chicago Press
Chicago and London

Rudolf A. Makkreel is professor of philosophy at Emory University. He is the author of *Dilthey: Philosopher of the Human Studies* and coeditor of Wilhelm Dilthey's *Selected Works* (in progress).

The University of Chicago Press, Chicago 60637
The University of Chicago Press, Ltd., London
© 1990 by The University of Chicago
All rights reserved. Published 1990
Printed in the United States of America
99 98 97 96 95 94 93 92 91 90   5 4 3 2 1

Library of Congress Cataloging-in-Publication Data

Makkreel, Rudolf A.
    Imagination and interpretation in Kant : the hermeneutical import
of the Critique of judgment / Rudolf A. Makkreel.
        p.   cm.
    Includes bibliographical references.
    ISBN 0-226-50276-7 (alk. paper)
        1. Kant, Immanuel, 1724–1804.   Kritik der Urteilskraft.   2. Kant,
Immanuel, 1724–1804—Contributions in hermeneutics.
    3. Hermeneutics.   4. Judgment (Logic).   5. Aesthetics.   6. Teleology.
    I. Title.
    B2784.M27   1990
    121—dc20   89-39715
                                                            CIP

To Frances

Contents

Preface

In this book I have brought together my long-standing interests in imagination and interpretation by developing Kant's theory of reflective judgment. Because the imagination is a power that both exhibits and overcomes the limits of experience, its study is relevant to hermeneutics as well as to epistemology and aesthetics. Interpretation must also cope with the limits of our discursive understanding and, like the imagination, is essential in relating what is directly given in experience to what is only indirectly given.

The interpretive potential of the imagination can be brought out through the theory of reflective judgment introduced in Kant's *Critique of Judgment*. In the *Critique of Pure Reason* the imagination served the constitutive demands of the understanding and the regulative ideals of reason. But the role of the imagination is expanded in relation to the reflective tasks of aesthetic and teleological judgments. To recognize the hermeneutic implications of these reflective judgments it is necessary to understand that they are not, as is often supposed, synthetic in nature and do not simply make the kind of regulative or heuristic projections about nature already found in the Dialectic of the *Critique of Pure Reason*. Nor does reflection for Kant involve a turning in upon the self. Reflective judgment involves a response to the content of the world; its transcendental principle is concerned with the specification and systematic organization of nature as a whole. By relating reflection to some of the nonsynthetic processes of the imagination, we can see that reflective judgment is essentially interpretive in nature.

This book is dedicated to my wife, Frances Tanikawa, who has been my most sympathetic critic throughout. I am deeply grateful for the time and thought she has given to editing my work—and for her love and support in all things.

I also would like to thank those with whom I have discussed the ideas that are developed in this book. They include Lewis White Beck, Richard Bernstein, Donald Crawford, Edward Mahoney, Joseph Margolis, Thomas Rockmore, and from Germany, Manfred Riedel, Thomas Seebohm, and Ludwig Siep. Others who have made helpful comments about earlier drafts include Wally Adamson, John Krois, Charles Nussbaum, and Charles Sherover.

Research support for this book includes grants from the Alexander von Humboldt Stiftung and the Emory University Research Committee. Finally, I want to acknowledge the assistance of Dennis Dugan and Virginia Jennings, as well as the encouraging support received from David Brent of the University of Chicago Press, Thomas Flynn and Donald Verene of Emory University.

Some earlier essays that anticipate the views developed in this book are "Imagination and Temporality in Kant's Theory of the Sublime," *Journal of Aesthetics and Art Criticism* 42 (Spring 1984): 303–15; "The Feeling of Life: Some Kantian Sources of Life-Philosophy," *Dilthey-Jahrbuch für Philosophie und Geschichte der Geisteswissenschaften* 3 (1985): 83–104; and "Tradition and Orientation in Hermeneutics," *Research in Phenomenology* 16 (1986): 73–85. My thanks to the journal editors for permission to republish parts of these essays.

Abbreviations

A	Baumgarten, *Aesthetica*
AP	*Anthropology from a Pragmatic Point of View*
C1	*Critique of Pure Reason*
C2	*Critique of Practical Reason*
C3	*Critique of Judgment*
CB	"Conjectural Beginning of Human History"
CF	*Conflict of the Faculties*
DSS	*Dreams of a Spirit-Seer*
FI	*First Introduction to the Critique of Judgment*
FPT	"On the Failure of All Attempted Philosophical Theodicies"
L	*Logic: A Manual for Lectures*
LE	*Lectures on Ethics*
M	Baumgarten, *Metaphysica*
MEJ	*Metaphysical Elements of Justice*
MFNS	*Metaphysical Foundations of Natural Science*
MPV	*Metaphysical Principles of Virtue*
OP	*Opus postumum*
PFM	*Prolegomena to Any Future Metaphysics*
RA	*Reflexionen zur Anthropologie*
RL	*Reflexionen zur Logik*
RM	*Reflexionen zur Metaphysik*
RWL	*Religion within the Limits of Reason Alone*
TP	*On the Old Saw: That May Be Right in Theory but It Won't Work in Practice*
UH	"Idea for a Universal History from a Cosmopolitan Point of View"
WIE	"What Is Enlightenment?"
WOT	"What Is Orientation in Thinking?"

Introduction

The role of the imagination in Kant's philosophy is most often discussed in terms of the synthetic functions assigned to it in the *Critique of Pure Reason,* where it serves the understanding in the constitution of experience. But in Kant's overall theory, the imagination displays a broader range of powers than is evident in the first *Critique.* Particularly, with the emergence of its reflective functions in the *Critique of Judgment,* the imagination can be shown to contribute to the interpretation, as well as to the constitution, of experience.

In tracing Kant's views on the imagination we will distinguish three phases in the development of his theory. In the precritical writings the imagination is described as having a variety of formative powers. While most of these are concerned with imaging, others point to functions that will be developed in the first and third *Critiques.* In the *Critique of Pure Reason,* Kant focuses on the imagination as a transcendental productive power providing a priori schemata that make possible the application of the categories to sense. At this stage its synthetic activities assist in the scientific understanding or "reading" of nature. Finally, in the *Critique of Judgment,* the powers of the imagination are extended in relation to reflective judgment and reason. Kant now ascribes to the imagination the power of aesthetic comprehension, and also the capacity to create aesthetic ideas by which it can present rational ideas to sense. Here the imagination, in conjunction with reflective judgment, displays the potential for what I will call a "reflective interpretation" of our world.

Although Kant did not work out an explicit theory of interpretation, his stress on the limits of the human understanding points to the need for interpretation in comprehending the coherence and significance of our experience. Neither the categories of the understanding nor the ideas of reason are innately or directly knowable, and must be related back to the contents of sense, which are directly given. Any philosophy that thus requires a mediation between what is directly and indirectly accessible in experience sets the stage for the hermeneutic process. As the faculty that mediates between sense on the one hand and understanding and reason on the other, the imagination serves not only the aims of the understanding in legislating to nature, but also the interests of reason and reflective judgment in interpreting the overall order of nature and history. Especially with Kant's move to a more holistic perspective in the third *Critique,* the imagination and reflective judgment can help us to draw out the hermeneutic implications of Kant's philosophy.

Kant has been given little serious consideration in contemporary discussions of hermeneutics, for his transcendental epistemology is thought to be incompatible with the hermeneutical claim that every starting point is subject to reinterpretation. In addition, many current writers follow Hans-Georg Gadamer in dismissing Kant's aesthetics as a source of the subjectivist nineteenth-century hermeneutics that has been superseded by a new philosophical hermeneutics based on Heidegger. Admittedly, Kant's work may appear hermeneutically irrelevant if the epistemology of the *Critique of Pure Reason* and the aesthetics of the *Critique of Judgment* are treated separately. However, when Kant's aesthetics is related to his larger epistemological concerns, it can contribute to a critical hermeneutics in which the transcendental standpoint is no longer conceived as exclusively foundational for a science of nature, but as orientational for the human subject in the world.

The effort to clarify and develop Kant's views on imagination and interpretation has led me to reconsider the role of the third *Critique* in the Kantian critical project. According to the standard view, the *Critique of Pure Reason* and the *Critique of Practical Reason* establish the parameters of Kant's system. The task of the *Critique of Judgment* then is merely to resolve tensions between theoretical and practical reason by showing not only that their respective domains of legislation are not incompatible, but also that they can be felt to be in harmony in aesthetic judgments. Those who evaluate the role of the third *Critique* in this manner will concur with Hegel that it is a failed attempt at synthesis. The subjective, even contingent, manner in which we find aesthetic and teleological order in nature does not suffice to demonstrate the doctrinal coherence of Kant's philosophical system.

Instead of regarding the third *Critique* as an attempt to synthesize the first two *Critiques,* I propose that it can provide an interpretive framework for them. In doing so, I take seriously Kant's assertion that the *Critique of Judgment* is not intended to make a contribution to doctrinal philosophy. Unlike the first two *Critiques,* which ground the doctrinal metaphysical systems of natural science and morals, the *Critique of Judgment* has no specific metaphysical application. It deals with the harmony of the cognitive faculties and examines the conditions for the systematization of all knowledge. The work turns from the doctrinal claims of determinant judgment in the first two *Critiques* to a reflective mode of judgment whose function is interpretive rather than legislative.

Whereas determinant judgments are defined as proceeding from given universals (concepts) to particulars, reflective judgments attempt to find universals (ideas) for given particulars. In the former case, judgment is controlled by the pure concepts of either the understanding or reason. The reflective judgment, however, is more free from external control and allows the imagination to create its own ideas for organizing experience as a formally purposive system. The systematization of nature, which is achieved only hypothetically in the first *Critique* through the regulative use of rational ideas, is now justified by a transcendental principle of reflective judgment which can have both constitutive and regulative applications. Through the reflective principle of purposiveness and the introduction of aesthetic, normal, and teleological ideas of the imagination, the third *Critique* opens up a broader, interpretive context than was evident in the first *Critique.* From this perspective, the *Critique of Judgment* can be used to arrive at theoretical presuppositions that have not been uncovered in the *Critique of Pure Reason*—without, however, undermining any of its cognitive claims.

A few attempts have been made to extend Kant's theory of reflective judgment beyond the problems of taste and purposiveness in nature that are explicitly addressed in the *Critique of Judgment.* Most notably, Hannah Arendt has applied the reflective conditions of aesthetic judgment to the analysis of political judgment and community.[1] My aim here is to draw out the implications of reflective judg-

---

1. See Hannah Arendt, *Lectures on Kant's Political Philosophy,* ed. Ronald Beiner (Chicago: University of Chicago Press, 1982). See also the writings of Beiner, Howard, Lyotard, and Vollrath in the bibliography.

ment for the more general epistemological and hermeneutical problems of human inquiry.

This work is divided into three parts. Parts 1 and 2 focus on the development of Kant's theory of the imagination in an attempt to
reassess its well-known synthetic functions and bring to light the
other formative and reflective functions that have been overlooked.
In part 3, I amplify and extend Kant's reflections on imagination and
interpretation for a possible application beyond their original intent.
Since my purpose is to develop the resources within Kantian philosophy, I have made use of Kant's concepts and language as much as
possible instead of displaying their "relevance" by retrospectively imposing the terminology and viewpoints of later hermeneutical theories.

Chapter 1 deals with the imagination (*Einbildungskraft*) and the
many other modes of formative power (*Bildungskraft*) that Kant introduces in his early writings. Heidegger's attempt to relate three of
these formative powers to the three syntheses of the Subjective Deduction in the first *Critique* is criticized for failing to distinguish the
synoptic and spatial features of formation from the temporal features
of synthesis. In chapter 2, I also consider the imagination's role in the
Objective Deduction and then in the revised Deduction of the B edition. In the latter, the renaming of imaginative synthesis as "figurative" recalls several of the imagination's formative powers, especially
in relation to the production of monograms for mathematical figures.
Although some have considered the imagination to be interpretive in
the first *Critique,* I argue that its schematizing function there assigns
objective meanings to the categories as part of a rather fixed but general reading of nature, one which still lacks the flexibility and
specificity that we normally demand of interpretation.

Part 2, "The Imagination in the *Critique of Judgment,*" examines
the ways in which the imagination's role changes when Kant turns to
reflective judgment and the conditions of aesthetic consciousness
and mental life as a whole. It is argued in chapter 3 that in relation to
reflective judgment the functions of the imagination are no longer
conceived in terms of the synthesis of representations (*Vorstellungen*).
The aesthetic apprehension of a beautiful form does not begin with
temporally discrete representations, which must then be synthesized,
but with an indeterminate sense of a whole. In relation to the search
for systematic order of reflective judgment, the imagination is dis-

cussed as the faculty of presentation (*Darstellung*) that makes possible the reflective specification of nature as a whole in terms of a harmoniously coexisting system of genera and species.

In chapter 4, on the sublime, the imagination is related to reason rather than to the understanding, and is shown to overcome the sequential, linear form of time that is assumed in the first *Critique*. We see the imagination's power extended from apprehension to an aesthetic comprehension in which it is able to instantaneously grasp multiplicity as a unity. This leads to a discussion of the more holistic approach of the third *Critique* and the possibility of a transcendental philosophy of mind with a more integrated view of the subject.

Chapter 5 focuses on the idea of life in the third *Critique*. Although Kant's explicit references to the feeling of life in aesthetic judgments have gone virtually unnoticed, I argue that life is a pervasive theme underlying both the aesthetic and teleological halves of the *Critique of Judgment*. The feeling of life not only exhibits a responsiveness that indicates a modification of Kant's psychological assumptions, but also provides an overall perspective for interpreting the reflective functions of the imagination.

In part 3, entitled "Judgment and Reflective Interpretation," I make use of ideas produced by the imagination to suggest a theory of "reflective interpretation," which is to be distinguished from Kant's systematic interpretation of nature based on ideas of reason alone. Whereas systematic interpretation proceeds architectonically on the basis of fixed rational rules, reflective interpretation proceeds tectonically on the basis of revisable and indeterminate guidelines. Here interpretation becomes hermeneutical because the parts of a given whole are used to enrich and specify our initial understanding of it.

In chapter 6, I deal with the normal and aesthetic ideas of the imagination, which serve an interpretive function as indirect presentations of archetypes of nature and rational ideas. Aesthetic ideas add to our interpretation of experience by suggesting significant affinities even when direct conceptual connections are lacking.

In chapter 7, some of Kant's speculations in his popular writings about purposiveness in history are brought into the critical framework by reconceiving them as reflective teleological judgments. The notion of authentic interpretation, derived from Kant's discussions of religious hermeneutics, points to a reflective moral interpretation of culture and history. Finally, it is in chapter 8 that I argue that the transcendental conditions of reflective judgment are orientational rather than foundational and thus compatible with the hermeneutical standpoint. The conditions needed for judgment to "orient itself" must be supplemented with the synoptic power of the imagination suggested in the precritical writings and the *sensus communis* appealed to in the *Critique of Judgment* if valid reflective interpretations of the world are to be possible. The *sensus communis,* which Kant claims to be a presupposition for the communicability of all knowledge, enlarges our perspective on the world and helps to establish a framework for reflecting on both the human and the natural sciences.

Part One

The Imagination:
Precritical and Critical

I

Image Formation and Synthesis: from the Precritical Writings to the *Critique of Pure Reason*

Kant's most noted contribution to the theory of the imagination was to show its epistemological role in the constitution of experience. His insight in the *Critique of Pure Reason* that the imagination performs a transcendental task in schematizing concepts of the understanding and connecting the intuitive contents of sense gave the imagination a respectability it had never had before. The literature on Kant's theory of imagination has thus been largely devoted to this synthesizing function in the service of the understanding.

An examination of Kant's precritical writings will show, however, that Kant first considered a much broader range of functions for the imagination—only some of which were developed in the *Critique of Pure Reason,* while others can be related to the activities of the imagination in the *Critique of Judgment*. In this chapter I will survey the many formative powers initially associated with the imagination, and then compare three of them to the three syntheses of the Subjective Deduction of the *Critique of Pure Reason*. Since Heidegger has already covered some of this ground, an evaluation of his views will help to differentiate my own approach to the imagination in the first *Critique*.

The Formative Powers in the "Reflections on Anthropology"

The Cartesian tradition had generally mistrusted the imagination as an arbitrary sensory power and a source of error. However, Leibniz created a more favorable climate in Germany for a reevaluation of the imagination with his dynamic conception of perceptions as striving to preserve and complete themselves. Thus Christian Wolff and A. G. Baumgarten gave detailed discussions of the imagination in their treatments of empirical psychology. Inspired by Wolff's psychology, the Swiss critics Bodmer and Breitinger were among the first in the

German context to stress the importance of the imagination for poetry.

Kant's precritical reflections on the imagination were much influenced by Wolff and, especially, Baumgarten.[1] Wolff called the imagination the "power to poeticize or invent (*erdichten*),"[2] and in Alfred Baeumler's view Wolff anticipated Kant's productive imagination by allowing the imagination to invent new shapes and create mathematical constructions.[3] Wolff also pointed out that it is easier for the imagination to reproduce abstract forms and shapes than to reproduce colors. This gave the imagination a formal significance that Kant would develop further.

Kant's early views on the imagination are more readily compared with Baumgarten's work. For his lectures on metaphysics, Kant repeatedly used Baumgarten's *Metaphysica* (1739) as his text—including the part devoted to empirical psychology. There Baumgarten discusses the lower cognitive faculties in relation to the perfection of sensory knowledge. Subsequently, in his *Aesthetica* (1750–58), he states that the perfection of sensory knowledge is equivalent to the appreciation and production of beauty.[4] This claim is associated with the modern meaning given by Baumgarten to the term "aesthetics." To the older usage concerning the study of sensibility, he added the new meaning of aesthetics as the science of beauty and taste. Baumgarten retained the ancient tie between beauty and truth, but he revised it by connecting beauty to sensory, as distinct from conceptual, knowledge. As the science of the perfection of sensory knowledge, aesthetics is not merely subservient to the science of conceptual knowledge. It does more than supply the sensory content for the traditional, abstract logic of concepts; it develops its own logic for the "complete determination of the singular,"[5] which is the proper perfection of percepts. According to this new perceptual logic, sense can exhibit not only the *intensive clarity* of the distinct qualities of things,

1. Johann Tetens influenced Kant in a later stage of his development. See chapter 6.

2. Christian Wolff, *Vernünftige Gedancken von Gott, der Welt und der Seele des Menschen* (Hildesheim: Georg Olms Verlag, 1983), §242, 135.

3. Cf. Alfred Baeumler, *Das Irrationalitätsproblem in der Ästhetik und Logik des 18. Jahrhunderts bis zur "Kritik der Urteilskraft"* (Darmstadt: Wissenschaftliche Buchgesellschaft, 1974), 146.

4. See A. G. Baumgarten, *Aesthetica* (hereafter *A*) (Hildesheim: Georg Olms, 1970), §14.

5. Mary J. Gregor, "Baumgarten's *Aesthetica*," *Review of Metaphysics* 37 (1983): 364.

but also the *extensive clarity* of a concrete whole as perceived in a single glance. Here Baumgarten raises the problem of instantaneously grasping a whole, which Kant will address in various ways through the power of the imagination. (See, for example, the discussions of synopsis in this chapter and of the *Augenblick* in chapter 4.)

We know from the *Critique of Pure Reason* (*C1*, A21/B35–36) that Kant at first resisted Baumgarten's new beauty-related use of the term "aesthetics." He later adopted it in the *Critique of Judgment* (*C3*, §15), but without accepting Baumgarten's ideas of "aestheticological truth" (*A*, §556) and of beauty as a kind of perfection. However, there is no doubt that Kant's own precritical reflections on the powers of sense and the imagination were greatly influenced by Baumgarten's account of the representational powers of the lower cognitive faculties. According to the *Metaphysica*, the cultivation of sensory knowledge requires (1) *acute sentiendi*, the ability to sense or perceive acutely,[6] (2) *phantasia*, the power to "reproduce" images (*M*, §559), and (3) *perspicacia*, the power of penetrating insight (*M*, §573). It is in relation to *perspicacia* that Baumgarten discusses the play of wit which constantly fascinated Kant (*M*, §576). The perfection of sensory knowledge also demands (4) *memoria*, which allows us not merely to reproduce but to "recognize" past representations (*M*, §579), (5) the *facultas fingendi*, the power of the imagination to invent (*M*, §589), and (6) *praevisio*, the capacity to imagine the future (*M*, §595). It is in the context of the next power, (7) *judicium* or judgment, that Baumgarten addresses the question of the "formation of taste" (*formandi gustum*), saying that "sensitive judgment is taste in the wider sense" (*M*, §607). The next mode of sensory knowledge involves (8) *praesagitio*, the capacity to foretell the future through the expectation of similarities (*M*, §612), which prepares the way for (9) the *facultas characteristica*, the power to represent through signs (*M*, §619).[7]

6. See A. G. Baumgarten, *Metaphysica* (hereafter *M*) (Hildesheim: Georg Olms, 1963), §540.

7. In the *Aesthetica*, Baumgarten discusses essentially the same representational capacities given in the *Metaphysica*. However, the inventive imagination (*facultas fingendi*) and the reproductive imagination (*phantasia*) are merged as aspects of a poetic disposition (*dispositio poetica*) (*A*, §34). In §22 of the *Aesthetica*, Baumgarten specifies that knowledge provided by the artist must display abundance, magnitude, truth, clarity, certitude, and liveliness. Ernst Cassirer interprets the last characteristic, liveliness, to be the key feature of Baumgarten's aesthetic knowledge. "The power and greatness of the artist," Cassirer writes, "consists in his ability to endow the 'cold symbols' of the language of daily life and of the language of science with the breath of life, with the 'life

The most interesting feature of Kant's treatment of Baumgarten's lower cognitive faculties is the move toward a more unified conception of their various representational functions. Kant's *Reflexionen zur Anthropologie* consist of fragmentary notes and comments related to Baumgarten's *Metaphysica*, but taken together they suggest that all the lower cognitive faculties may be viewed as aspects of a general formative faculty, or *Bildungsvermögen*. The formative power that Baumgarten brings out only in relation to (7) judgment and the formation of taste is applied by Kant to all the representational functions of sense by construing them as modes of *Bildung* (formation). Thereby formation becomes the most pervasive feature of all modes of intuiting and imaging.

A *Bildungsvermögen* is most clearly displayed in the formation of an image (*Bild*), but, as described in *Reflexion* 331,[8] this formative faculty also encompasses the power to coordinate representations in general.[9] The relation between form and coordination is clarified in Kant's reflections on logical and aesthetic perfection where Kant writes, "Form for the *objectis sensuum* is coordination, form for the *objectis rationis* is subordination."[10] Whereas subordination is a logical mode of form, coordination is an aesthetic mode of form corresponding to Baumgarten's extensive clarity. The distinction between the logical form of subordination and the aesthetic form of coordination will be related to the distinction between determinant and reflective judgment in chapter 3.

Kant makes it clear that the formative faculty is active in perceptual

of knowledge' (*vita cognitionis*)" (Ernst Cassirer, *The Philosophy of the Enlightenment,* trans. F. C. A. Koelln and J. P. Pettegrove [Princeton: Princeton University Press, 1951], 350). When we turn to the *Critique of Judgment,* we will see that liveliness as an aesthetic perfection is developed in the idea of aesthetic pleasure as the feeling of the enhancement of life (see chapter 5).

    8. Immanuel Kant, *Reflexionen zur Anthropologie* (hereafter *RA*), no. 331, in *Gesammelte Schriften, herausgegeben von der Preussischen Akademie der Wissenschaften zu Berlin,* 29 vols. (Berlin: Walter de Gruyter, 1902–83), XV, 130. Hereafter all references to this Academy edition will simply use Roman numerals to designate volume numbers. Reflection 331 is thought to stem from the period between 1776–78. Henceforth I will list the most likely dates of reflections after their page numbers. For the method of dating Kant's reflections see XIV, xxxv–xlvii.

    9. Kant speaks of a *facultas formatrix* as belonging to the *Bildungsvermögen*. The tectonic formative faculty coordinates representations by proceeding from part to whole; the architectonic formative faculty proceeds from a whole to its parts (see *RA*, 332; XV, 131; 1776–78).

    10. Kant, *Reflexionen zur Logik* (hereafter *RL*), no. 1799; XVI, 119; 1769–75.

as well as imaginative processes, i.e., "either in relation to given or nongiven objects" (*RA,* 332; XV, 131; 1776–78). When the formative faculty (*Bildungsvermögen*) is used only in relation to given objects it is called a *Bildungskraft,* which is the power to coordinate or give form to intuitions. When used in relation to nongiven objects, it is called *Einbildung,* the power of imaginative formation. Kant writes: "Imaginative formation (*Einbildung*) can be distinguished from the power to give form to an intuition (*Bildungskraft*) in that it makes images without the presence of an object (admittedly from the materials of sense), either by invention (*fingendo*) or by abstraction (*abstrahendo*)" (*RA,* 330; XV, 130; 1776–78). Kant's *Einbildung* displays both the inventive power of Baumgarten's *facultas fingendi* and the power of abstraction emphasized by Wolff. It reflects Baumgarten's concern for the concrete as well as Wolff's interest in form.

In addition to *Bildungskraft* and *Einbildung* Kant mentions several other modes of *Bildung.* They appear in different *Reflexionen,* but each can be interpreted as a species of the generic formative faculty (*Bildungsvermögen*). *Abbildung* (direct image formation), *Nachbildung* (reproductive image formation), and *Vorbildung* (anticipatory image formation) are three such modes of *Bildung* roughly corresponding to the functions in Baumgarten of acute perception (1), reproductive *phantasia* (2), and *praevisio* (6). According to Kant, *Abbildung,* "the power to depict a present, sensuous object, is fundamental" (*RA,* 315; XV, 125; 1769). *Abbildung* "exhibits" what is given to the senses in an image, which in turn "informs" the images of *Nachbildung* and *Vorbildung* (see *RA,* 336, 313a; XV, 133, 123; 1776–78, 1769). Direct, reproductive, and anticipatory image formation are claimed by Kant to be temporally definable (*RA,* 329; XV, 130; 1776–78). The first forms an empirical image of the present, the second of the past, the third of the future.

According to Kant, two other modes of *Bildung* are not temporally definable. *Ausbildung* is that mode of formation which completes images, *Gegenbildung* that which allows images to serve as linguistic signifiers or symbolic analogues for something else. In *Reflexion* 313a (XV, 123; 1769) Kant speaks of the imagination producing a "*Gegenbild : symbolum,*" a counterimage that serves as a linguistic analogue.[11] The imaginative capacity of *Gegenbildung* is related to Baumgarten's

11. The specific term *Gegenbildung* appears in the lectures on metaphysics transcribed by Pölitz. There *Gegenbildung* is defined as the "Vermögen der Charakteristik" (XXVIII, 237) that operates "per analogiam" (XXVIII, 238).

facultas characteristica, the power to represent by means of signs (see *RA,* 326; XV, 129; 1769–70). *Ausbildung* can be called completing formation, and *Gegenbildung* analogue or symbolic formation.

Finally, Kant suggests the possibility of adding *Urbildung* as another variation, when he describes genius as an *"urbildende Talent,"* i.e., a "talent for the formation of archetypes" (see *RA,* 533; XV, 232; 1776–79). In another *Reflexion* he writes that "we draw finally from all objects of one type an archetype (*Urbild*)" (*RA,* 323; XV, 127; 1769–70). We can thus call *Urbildung* the power of archetypal formation.

The different species of *Bildungsvermögen* suggested in the precritical *Reflexionen* can now be summarized as follows:

1. *Bildung:* coordinating or giving form to intuition

---

2. *Abbildung:* direct image formation
3. *Nachbildung:* reproductive image formation
4. *Vorbildung:* anticipatory image formation
5. *Einbildung:* imaginative formation
6. *Ausbildung:* completing formation
7. *Gegenbildung:* analogue or symbolic formation

---

8. *Urbildung:* archetypal formation

Functions 1 and 8, *Bildung* and *Urbildung,* have been separated off because they do not involve the imagination, but are modes of giving form to intuition. *Bildung* deals with human sensible intuition and *Urbildung* implies a form of intellectual intuition rejected in the critical writings. Functions 2–7 represent various processes of imaging or imagining; *Abbildung, Nachbildung,* and *Vorbildung* (2–4) are modes of empirical image formation related to the *Imagination*—the German term used for the imagination when it is conceived as the "storehouse (*Vorrath*) of representations" (*RA,* 334; XV, 132; 1776–78).

I have arranged the species of the *Bildungsvermögen* in a sequence that reflects their relative degree of dependence on the material world. The power to coordinate or give form to intuitions (*Bildungskraft*) and direct image formation (*Abbildung*) leave the subject quite dependent on a present object. *Nachbildung* and *Vorbildung* involve the generation of images according to empirical laws of association and thus still reflect the material world in a general way. Yet, no matter how dependent on the empirical object, the formation of images never renders a mere passive copy. *Einbildung* or imaginative formation is the first to constitute a less dependent mode of formation. The power to invent images, initiated by *Einbildung* and developed by *Ausbildung* and *Gegenbildung* (5–7), shows the subject to have the capacity for voluntary transformations. Imaginative formation, says Kant, "does not have its cause in real representation, but arises from an activity of the soul" (*RA*, 314; XV, 124; 1769). This suggests that an independent causal source, manifested in what Kant regards as the life force of the soul,[12] is introduced with *Einbildung*. However, Kant also asserts that even the invented image (*Erdichtung*) derives its content from the senses. We cannot produce images ex nihilo; only their form can be new. Formation seems to involve a largely causal conception of mind that is neither wholly dependent on, nor fully independent of, the material world.

Kant hints that *Einbildung* sometimes functions unconsciously: "It loves to wander in the dark" (*RA*, 312; XV, 121; 1766–68). But when imaginative formation operates consciously, it becomes a mode of invention (*Erdichtung*) that "connects all representations by a free act of volition" (*RA*, 314; XV, 124; 1769). Here Kant raises the synthetic or connecting function that will be the central role of the imagination in the *Critique of Pure Reason*. However, in these early writings, it is but one of various tasks that is assigned to the imagination and is most often discussed with reference to analogue or symbolic formation (see *RA*, 322, 326; XV, 127, 129; 1769–70, 1769–70).

Synoptic Formation in the "Lectures on Metaphysics"

A further view of the imagination as a formative power of sense is provided in Kant's *Vorlesungen über Metaphysik* (Lectures on Metaphysics). The set of lectures that Kant is thought to have delivered in 1778–79 or 1779–80[13] includes some of his most extensive discussions of the different modes of *Bildung*. They provide evidence of what Kant was thinking just prior to the time when he finally made the breakthrough associated with the Subjective Deduction of the *Critique of Pure Reason*.[14] The lectures on metaphysics have been

12. For a less speculative conception of the relation between the imagination and the idea of life, see chapter 5.

13. Entitled "Metaphysik L_1: Kosmologie, Psychologie, Theologie nach Pölitz," XXVIII, 193–350.

14. See Norman Kemp Smith, *A Commentary on Kant's "Critique of Pure Reason,"* 2d ed. (New York: Humanities Press, 1962).

preserved through student notes and therefore are not completely authoritative. Nonetheless, they are useful for explicating ideas that Kant himself set forth in the *Reflexionen* and his published writings because he often provides more detailed analyses and concrete examples in his course lectures than in his written works.

In the lectures on metaphysics Kant emphasizes the three modes of image formation that foreshadow the three syntheses of the Subjective Deduction of the *Critique of Pure Reason*. These are the elementary modes of the *Bildungsvermögen*: direct image formation (*Abbildung*), whose representations are of the present; reproductive image formation (*Nachbildung*), which represents the past; and anticipatory image formation (*Vorbildung*), which anticipates the future. Kant explicitly states that while these elementary modes of image formation are imitative and dependent on how our senses are affected by objects, they are nevertheless actively formative.

The most detailed account of the activity involved in *Bildung* is devoted to *Abbildung*, or direct image formation. "My mind is always busy in forming an image of the manifold by surveying it," Kant writes. "For example, if I see a city, the mind forms an image of the object which it has before it, by running through (*durchläuft*) its manifold" (XXVIII, 235). In describing what is involved in *Abbildung* Kant emphasizes that the mind seeks to do justice to the complexity and totality of the object at hand:

> The mind must undertake to make many observations to form a direct image of an object. This is because it forms a different image from every side. A city, for example, looks different from the morning aspect than from the evening aspect. There are many different appearances of a thing from different sides and viewpoints. From all these appearances, the mind must make itself an image by gathering them together (*zusammen nimmt*). (XXVIII, 236)

The phrases "running through" and "gathering together" anticipate the language used to describe the synthesis of apprehension in the *Critique of Pure Reason*, A99 (see IV, 77). The discussion of *Abbildung* also contains elements that will reappear in the *Critique of Judgment* when Kant deals with aesthetic comprehension. Both direct image formation and aesthetic comprehension run into difficulties when our impressions are so overpowering that we do not know where to begin gathering the manifold. In the lectures on metaphysics Kant cites the example of someone's being overwhelmed as he enters St. Peter's Basilica in Rome for the first time. He refers to the same case in the *Critique of Judgment* to illustrate the limits of aesthetic comprehension in the sublime (see chapter 4).

An *Abbild* is not a mere causal effect produced by an object. Although the image actively formed by the mind is of an object in the present, the image encompasses more than the present. We saw in the preceding passage that our mental image of a city must include not only the "morning aspect (*Morgenseite*)," but also the "evening aspect (*Abendseite*)." Kant speaks of these aspects as if they were only spatial perspectives. But he goes on to say: "The present appearance (*Erscheinung*) contains representations of past and future time" (XX-VIII, 236). This means that the *Abbildung* of a present appearance is not as direct a mode of image formation as Kant initially indicated. It is really what I would call a "synoptic" formation that incorporates past and future representations into a present image. Although Kant continues to treat the three processes of image formation as essentially distinct, with each focusing on either the present, the past, or the future, his example of the synoptic city image seems to blur these temporal differences and suggests that *Abbildung* cannot fulfill its task without the cooperation of reproductive and anticipatory image formation.

As noted earlier, all three modes of elementary image formation are related to the *Imagination,* which Kant characterizes as the storehouse of our representations. The *Imagination,* unlike *Einbildung* (imaginative formation), operates according to empirical laws of association. The process of *Vorbildung* that forms an image of the future is not really productive, but relies on the same reproductive laws of association that explain *Nachbildung*. When we reproduce a past representation or anticipate a future representation we are reviving images that have been derived from experience and stored in the *Imagination*. The only difference then between *Nachbildung* and *Vorbildung* is that one moves from past to present and the other from the past and present to the future—but in both cases by the predictable "laws of *Imagination*" (XXVIII, 236), otherwise known as the laws of association. In the *Reflexionen, Abbildung* was defined as the most fundamental mode of image formation. Being direct, it provided the content of the *Imagination* but did not seem to depend on its laws of association. But if it is to be capable of forming synoptic images that include past and future representations, *Abbildung* must also rely on the reproductive processes involved in *Nachbildung* and *Vorbildung*.

If all three modes of image formation involve a form of reproductive association, the question then becomes, On what basis can we continue to differentiate them? Kant always speaks of reproduction as a process that moves with the progressive sequence of the time line— we reproduce a representation from time 1 in time 2. Yet, this process can be appropriated by consciousness in either of two ways: (1) a past experience can be focused on for its own sake, as in memory, or (2) it can be integrated as a component of a present experience. The difference between the two can be conceived as one of intentional direction of consciousness. The first case represents *Nachbildung* as a distinct process of recollection, which is directed back to the past. In the second case, interest is directed toward the present and *Nachbildung* becomes part of the synoptic formation of *Abbildung*. This is discernible in the lectures where Kant describes *Nachbildung* from the point of view of the present as "recalling representations from previous times and connecting them with representations of the present" (XXVIII, 236). Similarly, *Vorbildung* can be either differentiated from or included in *Abbildung* by means of intentional direction. In itself *Vorbildung* points ahead to the future in terms of expectations extrapolated from the past and present. But as part of the process of *Abbildung*, *Vorbildung* is incorporated as an anticipatory aspect of our present synoptic image. Reproduction and anticipatory image formation become aspects of direct image formation when the concern of the latter is to give an overview, as in Kant's example of the image of the city. Most of the perspectives incorporated into the *Abbild* of the city cannot actually be sensed in the present and must therefore be imagined.[15]

Although what is present in perception does not suffice for the synoptic image of the city, all the other contents contained in the *Abbild* are derived from what was once present in perception and is now stored in the *Imagination*. Only with imaginative formation (*Ein-*

---

15. On this point we can see affinities with Merleau-Ponty's insight that the perception of an object includes not only what is directly given of the front side, but also what we imagine the back side to be like. Generally, Kant's view of the imagination is closer to Merleau-Ponty's than to Sartre's, which draws the sharpest possible contrast between perception and imagination. In Kant there are so many functions of the imagination that some of them overlap with perception (see *C1*, A120, n. a.).

bildung) can the spontaneity of the imagination begin to exhibit itself. *Einbildung* is defined in the lectures on metaphysics as "the faculty of producing images out of themselves (*aus sich selbst*) independently of the reality of objects" (XXVIII, 237). *Ausbildung* and *Gegenbildung* are the two further modes of imagination that can depart from what is given to it in intuition. *Ausbildung*, or completing formation, comes into play when the things we perceive "seem to be incomplete or imperfect" (XXVIII, 237). The imagination then projects "an idea of the whole" (XXVIII, 237) to round off and perfect what is found lacking in experience. However, when the lack stems not from what is perceived, but from the limits of our own intuiting powers, *Gegenbildung*, or analogue formation, becomes necessary. It forms symbolic analogues to produce indirect links between sense and reason where direct links are unavailable (see XXVIII, 238). These themes introduced in relation to *Ausbildung* and *Gegenbildung* in Kant's lectures on metaphysics give an early indication of the imagination's potential for interpretation and will be taken up again in the *Critique of Judgment* (see especially chapter 6).

Abbildung provides an interesting starting point because it illustrates that even the most direct empirical images are formed. Interpreted as synoptic formation, *Abbildung* can no longer be considered as the most fundamental mode of image formation. Nevertheless, it may be said to play a kind of orientational role when it is discussed in relation to the initial disorientation caused by the overwhelming size of certain objects. A synoptic image of the city can serve to orient us in representing its various aspects.[16]

Because what is given together in an *Abbildung* is focused on the present, but not literally restricted to it, Hermann Mörchen has observed that here the present (*Gegenwart*) does not refer to a mode of time, but to the spatial presence of an object.[17] This point is important to keep in mind as we turn to the discussion of the syntheses of the imagination in the *Critique of Pure Reason*. It accounts for the difference between the language of synoptic formation, which has spatial connotations, and the language of imaginative synthesis, which will be couched in temporal terms.

---

16. For more on orientation in relation to the imagination see chapter 8.

17. See Hermann Mörchen, *Die Einbildungskraft bei Kant* (Tübingen: Max Niemeyer Verlag, 1970), 15.

The Three Syntheses of the "Critique of Pure Reason"

In the *Critique of Pure Reason* the task of gathering representations becomes a task set for all representational consciousness because of the temporal nature of inner sense. The successive order in which the contents of inner sense are represented requires the mind to produce synthetic connections among its discrete representations. These syntheses may be empirical, but fundamentally they are transcendental and produce a unity which is derived from the spontaneity of the mind. A synthesis produced by the imagination is no longer discussed as a function of *Imagination* but as one of *Einbildungskraft*.

In the first edition (1781) of the *Critique of Pure Reason* Kant provides a preliminary Subjective Deduction of knowledge before going on to the Objective Deduction of the categories necessary for knowledge. There are, according to Kant, three subjective sources of knowledge: intuitive apprehension, imaginative reproduction, and conceptual recognition. Each has a transcendental synthesis associated with it, the first a synthesis by which various impressions of sense are apprehended as one manifold, the second a synthesis by which past representations are reproduced in a present manifold, and the third a synthesis which recognizes past and present representations as connected.

In order to explicate the role of these three syntheses and their relation to the imagination I will make reference to Heidegger's well-known interpretation of them in his *Kant and the Problem of Metaphysics*. Heidegger correlates the three syntheses with three of the elementary modes of image formation (*Bildung*) discussed earlier in this chapter. In doing so he assumes that all three syntheses are functions of the imagination, whereas Kant speaks of the imagination primarily when referring to the second synthesis of reproduction. Heidegger's comparisons are suggestive in highlighting the temporal character of the three syntheses, but they overlook an important shift in Kant's conception of the imagination that occurs as we move from the precritical writings to the *Critique of Pure Reason*.

Heidegger correlates the synthesis of apprehension with *Abbildung*, the synthesis of reproduction with *Nachbildung*, and the synthesis of recognition with *Vorbildung*.[18] Since Kant assigns one of the modes of time to each of the three empirical modes of image for-

18. Martin Heidegger, *Kant and the Problem of Metaphysics* (Bloomington: Indiana University Press, 1962), 180, 191.

mation, Heidegger uses the correlation to argue that the same holds for their supposed transcendental counterparts in the Subjective Deduction. But more significantly, he claims that each of these three syntheses is in some way time-forming. Thus he writes: "The pure synthesis as apprehension is, as presentative of the 'present in general', time-forming."[19] Similarly, "pure synthesis in the mode of reproduction forms the past as such."[20] Finally, the function of the pure synthesis of recognition involves what Heidegger calls a "prospecting" which "is the pure formation of that which makes all projection possible, i.e., the future."[21]

Heidegger makes the bold claim that all three syntheses are expressions of a transcendental imagination which he identifies with primordial time. "If the transcendental imagination as the pure formative faculty in itself forms time . . . then the thesis . . . that transcendental imagination *is* primordial time, can no longer be avoided."[22] He also argues that the transcendental imagination is what Kant sometimes refers to as the unknown common root uniting sense and understanding, the two stems of experience. According to Heidegger, Kant "recoiled from this unknown root" in the second edition (1787) of the *Critique of Pure Reason,* where the "transcendental imagination, as it was described in the vigorous language of the first edition, is thrust aside."[23]

In a review essay on Heidegger's *Kant and the Problem of Metaphysics,* Dieter Henrich has demonstrated that for Kant the common root is in principle unknowable and even in the first edition cannot be identified with the imagination or any other faculty. According to Henrich, such an interpretation makes sense only if we accept Heidegger's thesis in *Being and Time* that what unifies *Dasein* is a structure of equiprimordial moments.[24] But even if we were to accept the latter thesis, it could not be applied without distorting Kant's theory of the imagination. In the *Critique of Pure Reason,* the imagination provides only a functional unity for intuitions and concepts. A closer look at each of the three syntheses will show that some

19. Heidegger, *Kant,* 185.
20. Heidegger, *Kant,* 187.
21. Heidegger, *Kant,* 191.
22. Heidegger, *Kant,* 192, emphasis added.
23. Heidegger, *Kant,* 167.
24. Dieter Henrich, "Über die Einheit der Subjektivität," *Philosophische Rundschau,* vol. 3 (1955): 47, 62–69.

of Heidegger's more specific correlations with the three modes of image formation also cannot be upheld.

The first synthesis of the Subjective Deduction is labeled the "synthesis of apprehension in intuition." Every intuition, Kant writes, "contains in itself a manifold which would not be represented as a manifold if the mind did not distinguish time in the sequence of one impression upon another."[25] To become aware of the details of our sense experience we need to consider our impressions one at a time in inner sense. In the synthesis of apprehension these discrete impressions are "run through and gathered together" (*C1*, A99; IV, 77), thereby allowing us to represent them "as a manifold and as contained in a single representation" (*C1*, A99).

Although the language of "running through" and "gathering together" is reminiscent of Kant's description of *Abbildung,* there are certain key differences which differentiate synoptic image formation from the synthesis of apprehension. In the discussion of synoptic image formation the problem posed by the discreteness of the contents of inner sense was not yet raised, for *Abbildung* was really a process referring to outer sense and space. According to the *Critique of Pure Reason* all contents of outer sense are appropriated by inner sense and presented successively. The synthesis of apprehension makes it possible to bring together many impressions into one sequential manifold by relating them to the time continuum as the form of inner sense.

Kant speaks at first as if the time continuum by which we order sense impressions were a given. This is in accordance with Kant's treatment of time in the "Transcendental Aesthetic," where it is defined as "given a priori" (*C1*, A31/B46). But after exploring an empirical example of the syntheses of apprehension, Kant speaks of "a pure synthesis of apprehension" producing time (*C1*, A100). My a priori representation of time "can be produced only through the synthesis of the manifold which sensibility presents in its original receptivity" (*C1*, A99–100). Since, according to Kant, time exists only in my representation of it, this is equivalent to "my generating time *itself* in the apprehension of the intuition" (*C1*, A143/B182). Heidegger is thus quite right to claim that the pure synthesis of apprehension is "time-forming," but he misleadingly characterizes it as "presenta-

25. Kant, *Critique of Pure Reason* (hereafter *C1*), trans. Norman Kemp Smith (New York: St. Martin's Press, 1965), A99; IV, 77. When, as here, the Academy edition reference is added, this means that I have altered the translation.

tive of the 'present in general'."[26] Unlike the process of *Abbildung*, the synthesis of apprehension is not to be identified with the present, for this synthesis is necessary to assure the continuity of the different modalities of time. In the synoptic formation of *Abbildung*, past and future representations are incorporated in one present-oriented image. By contrast, the synthesis of apprehension spans a time continuum and therefore cannot be focused into one moment of time.

In the opening remarks of the Subjective Deduction, Kant himself points to a difference between synthesis and synopsis by treating the former as spontaneous and the latter as receptive. In what he calls a "synopsis" of sense, various impressions are received as parts of a whole (see *C1*, A97). Heidegger has proposed that instead of "synopsis" Kant should have used the term "syndosis," which means an original giving together that is simultaneous.[27] A synopsis, according to Heidegger, can mean that "I survey the manifold sequentially"[28] and thus implies a synthetic activity. Certainly, the synopsis in the foregoing interpretation of *Abbildung* involves more than the pure receptivity of Heidegger's syndosis or Kant's synopsis of sense. But the activity of synopsis is formative rather than synthetic or productive.

Kant's second synthesis, that of reproduction in imagination, deals even more explicitly with the temporality of inner sense and the fact that all representations are given successively. The reproductive image formation of *Nachbildung* was a purely empirical process of preserving past representations by means of the *Imagination* as the storehouse of representations. But in the *Critique of Pure Reason* Kant makes no such empirical assumption. Representations are not assumed to persist through time and must therefore be actively reproduced from one moment to the next. Kant writes: "When I seek to draw a line in thought . . . obviously the various manifold representations that are involved must be apprehended by me in thought one after the other. But if I were always to drop out of thought the preceding representations (the first parts of a line . . .), and did not reproduce them while advancing to those that follow, a complete representation would never be obtained" (*C1*, A102). It is the task of the

26. Heidegger, *Kant*, 185.

27. Heidegger, *Phänomenologische Interpretation von Kants "Kritik der reinen Vernunft," Gesamtausgabe*, vol. 25 (Frankfurt am Main: Vittorio Klostermann, 1977), 135.

28. Heidegger, *Phänomenologische Interpretation*, 135.

imagination, now conceived as *Einbildungskraft,* to reproduce past representations. Kant speaks of a transcendental synthesis whereby the imagination can associate past representations with present representations on the basis of a priori principles. Unlike *Nachbildung,* the synthesis of reproduction is not limited to one mode of time. It does not, as Heidegger says, "form the past as such," but allows us to revive the past in the present.

The third synthesis, the synthesis of recognition in a concept, is assigned two functions. The first deals with the recognition of sameness. Kant claims that "if we were not conscious that what we think is the same as what we thought a moment before, all reproduction in the series of representations would be useless. For it would in its present state be a new representation" (*CI,* A103). All imaginative reproduction would be in vain if we could not recognize what is reproduced at time 2 *as* a reproduction of what was first apprehended at time 1. The second function of the synthesis of recognition in a concept produces a unity among different representations. Thus the synthesis also makes it possible to unify the reproduced representations at time 2 and the newly apprehended representation at time 2. Only in this way can successive representations—as in the above example of the line—coexist as a unified whole. Kant illustrates this with a further example:

> If in counting, I forget that the units, which now hover before me, have been added to one another in succession, I should never know that a total is being produced through this successive addition of unit to unit, and so would remain ignorant of the number. For the concept of number is nothing but the consciousness of this unity of synthesis. (*CI,* A103)

Heidegger has correlated this synthesis of recognition with anticipatory image formation (*Vorbildung*), but the idea of "recognition (*Recognition*) in a concept" (*CI,* A103; IV, 79) is hardly directed at the future. Although concepts may be future-oriented rules, recognition in a concept involves a synthesis that unifies past and present representations. It is not comparable to *Vorbildung,* which projects the future on the basis of the law of association, because the third synthesis appeals to a transcendental principle even more fundamental than that found necessary for imaginative association in the second synthesis. But the synthesis of recognition does not provide a ground

for projecting primordial time. Instead, its transcendental function is
to produce a unity in temporal consciousness despite the fact that this
temporality of consciousness has a tendency to disperse the contents
of experience.

Finally, Heidegger's claim that the last synthesis "enjoys a priority
over the other two"[29] raises another point of contrast between the
three modes of empirical formation and the three syntheses. Among
the former, Kant declared the first mode, *Abbildung,* to be the most
fundamental. Although I have questioned whether this really holds for
Abbildung in the lectures on metaphysics, there is no way to justify the
view that *Vorbildung* is really most fundamental for Kant. The claim for
the priority of the synthesis of recognition in a concept must be based
on its being a function of the understanding rather than on Heidegger's interpretation of it as a mode of imagination projecting the future
as the primordial mode of time. The relationships among the three
syntheses is a complex question which we will consider in the next
chapter.

Although there are some parallels between the three elementary
modes of image formation (*Abbildung, Nachbildung,* and *Vorbildung*)
and the three syntheses of the Subjective Deduction, there are differences between them that are more significant for understanding
the development of Kant's theory of the imagination. The processes
of image formation in the precritical writings were conceived empirically and were dependent on the laws of association. The
syntheses of the *Critique of Pure Reason* are not merely formative in
the sense of extending, gathering, and elaborating images, but productive of the fundamental unities necessary for representations to
constitute experience.

As we now turn to a more detailed consideration of the role of
imaginative synthesis in the *Critique of Pure Reason,* we should not
lose sight of the fact that Kant did not always regard synthesis to be
the basic function of the imagination. When the role of the imagination is developed further in the *Critique of Judgment,* some of its
nonsynthetic functions discussed in the early writings will be appropriated in the critical framework.

29. Heidegger, *Kant,* 192.

2
The Figurative Synthesis of Imagination and the Meaning of Experience

We will now consider those aspects of the *Critique of Pure Reason* that are relevant to a recognition of the functions assigned to the imagination by the understanding. This requires us to reconcile claims about the imagination in the Subjective Deduction with the predominantly objective perspective of the second, or B, edition of the *Critique of Pure Reason*. The basic productive function of the imagination is there called a figurative synthesis. We will also examine how this synthesis relates to the basic transcendental process of schematizing the categories and what the imagination contributes to the meaning of experience in this process.

Imaginative Synthesis and the Understanding

In his initial formulation of the three syntheses in the Subjective Deduction, Kant remarks that representations "must all be ordered, connected and brought into relation in time." This, he tells us, must be "borne in mind" throughout the discussion of the three syntheses (see *C1*, A99). Here Kant may be taken to mean that the three syntheses can be placed in a *cumulative* sequence in which intuitive apprehension orders, imaginative reproduction connects, and conceptual recognition unifies. However, Kant's descriptions also suggest that the relationship among the three syntheses is *presuppositional*. The synthesis of apprehension is said to be "inseparably bound up with the synthesis of reproduction" (*C1*, A102), which itself "would be useless" without the synthesis of recognition (*C1*, A103).

Taken by itself, the Subjective Deduction provides grounds for both interpretations. Kant's assertion that our representations must be "ordered, connected and brought into relation" (A99) need not designate a cumulative sequence among the three syntheses, for ordering, connecting, and bringing into relation may be synonymous and expressions of a prior synthesis of recognition. Thus, reflecting the dominant view, H. J. Paton and A. C. Ewing contend that the three syntheses are only partial aspects of an overall conceptual synthesis.[1] According to Norman Kemp Smith, the movement from apprehension to reproduction to recognition actually reverses what is the case. He claims that in fact "reproduction conditions apprehension and both rest on recognition."[2]

However, it is also possible to maintain the cumulative thesis by regarding the synthesis of apprehension as a gathering synthesis, the synthesis of imaginative reproduction as an associative synthesis, and the synthesis of recognition as a connecting or unifying synthesis. Each synthesis then would be slightly more specific than its predecessor. There are also passages in the *Nachträge zur "Kritik der reinen Vernunft" (1. Auflage)* which show that, at least for a time, Kant held that a preconceptual transcendental synthesis of the imagination was possible. For example, in one entry Kant writes: "The transcendental synthesis of the imagination underlies all our concepts of the understanding" (XXIII, 18).[3] Using the expression "starting from below" in a later passage of the A Deduction (A119), Kant again suggests that apprehension is the basis for imaginative reproduction, which in turn prepares for recognition. Indeed his summary in the Objective Deduction appears to lend support to both the cumulative and presuppositional interpretations in the same passage: "Actual experience, which is constituted by apprehensions, association (reproduction), and *finally* recognition of appearances, contains in recognition, the *last and highest* of these merely empirical elements of experience, certain concepts which render possible the formal unity of experience, and therewith all objective validity (truth) of empirical knowledge" (*C1*, A124–25, emphases added). But then after identifying these concepts as the categories, Kant names the respective syntheses in reverse order: "Upon them [the categories] is based not only all formal unity in the synthesis of imagination, but also . . . all its empirical em-

1. See H. J. Paton, *Kant's Metaphysics of Experience* (London: George Allen & Unwin Ltd., 1965), vol. 1, 376; and A. C. Ewing, *A Short Commentary on Kant's "Critique of Pure Reason"* (Chicago: University of Chicago Press, 1967), 75.

2. Norman Kemp Smith, *A Commentary on Kant's "Critique of Pure Reason"* (see chap. 1, n. 14), 246.

3. Another passage makes the transcendental synthesis of the imagination the source of "the concept of an object in general" (XXIII, 18).

ployment (in recognition, reproduction, association, apprehension)"
(*C1*, A125; IV, 92).

Taken together the two sequences indicate a circular process. The
sequence beginning with apprehension provides the necessary content of experience, whereas the other, beginning with recognition,
provides its formal unity. Kant's formulation of the threefold synthesis as a sequence from below can only be accepted in terms of the
earlier language of formation (*Bildung*) that was associated with the
imagination in Kant's precritical writings. When apprehension, imaginative reproduction, and recognition within the overall view of
synthesis developed in the *Critique of Pure Reason* are discussed, the
sequence must begin with the synthesis of recognition. Ultimately all
synthesis is a function of the understanding and its categories. This is
the conclusion that Kant arrives at in the Objective Deduction.

Kant's final position that all intuitive and imaginative syntheses are
dependent on concepts of the understanding is even more clearly articulated in the B Deduction of the second edition of the *Critique of
Pure Reason*. There the Subjective Deduction is dropped so that the
understanding and its categories can be given a fundamental role from
the beginning. Kant writes at B130: "All combination—be we conscious of it or not, be it a combination of the manifold of intuition,
empirical or non-empirical, or of various concepts—is an act of the
understanding. To this act the general title 'synthesis' may be assigned." At B161 Kant asserts that all synthesis, "even that which
renders perception possible, is subject to the categories." This means
that all syntheses of apprehension are to be interpreted as empirical
applications of the transcendental synthesis made possible by the understanding. Kant is explicitly rejecting the view of the Subjective
Deduction that there can be transcendental syntheses of apprehension and reproduction independent of the categories. Now both
syntheses are considered as empirical applications of the categories.
However, Kant retains in the second edition what is probably the
most vigorous affirmation of his early view that the imagination is an
independent source of synthesis: "Synthesis in general, as we shall
hereafter see, is the mere result of the power of imagination, a blind
but indispensable function of the soul, without which we should have
no knowledge whatsoever, but of which we are scarcely ever conscious" (*C1*, A78/B103). Since this statement occurs in a preliminary
section of the Analytic that Kant did not revise, its retention in the

second edition can be explained as an oversight on Kant's part. The *Textemendationen* planned by Kant show that this sentence should have been changed so that the imagination would no longer be called "a blind but indispensable function of the soul." It is supposed to read: "Synthesis in general, as we shall hereafter see, is the mere result of the power of the imagination, a function of the understanding" (XXIII, 45). The syntheses performed by the imagination are undoubtedly dependent on the understanding.

Despite the fact that some of the claims of the Subjective Deduction cannot be upheld in the critical framework, it remains important for discerning the particular contributions made by the imagination in serving the understanding. Norman Kemp Smith has claimed that distinctions drawn in the Subjective Deduction between the different mental processes "are indispensably necessary in order to render really definite many of the contentions which the objective deduction itself contains."[4] The Subjective Deduction presents the most elaborate account of the temporal nature of our consciousness and how the various faculties cope with the discreteness of the contents of inner sense. Even acknowledging the understanding as the source of all synthesis, we cannot properly define the function of any act of synthesis, including that of the imagination, apart from the way inner sense is conceived in the Subjective Deduction.

Figurative Synthesis

So far we have mainly discussed image formation and the reproductive imagination in the Subjective Deduction. The central function of the imagination that is disclosed in the Objective Deduction is, however, productive. The *productive imagination* mediates between the understanding and sense to apply the transcendental unity of consciousness to "all objects of possible experience" (*C1*, A118). This involves a productive synthesis of the imagination which applies the categories of the understanding to sensibility.

In the B Deduction, Kant renames this transcendental synthesis of the imagination a "figurative synthesis (*synthesis speciosa*)" to distinguish it from the intellectual synthesis (*synthesis intellectualis*) of the understanding (*C1*, B151). "As figurative," Kant writes, "it is dis-

---

4. Kemp Smith, *A Commentary on Kant's "Critique of Pure Reason,"* 237.

tinguished from the intellectual synthesis, which is carried out by the understanding alone, without the aid of the imagination" (*CI*, B152). Kant gives no explicit reason why he chose to rename this synthesis a "figurative synthesis," but the term "figurative" aptly suggests the graphic, more spatial qualities that the imagination contributes to synthesis. Insofar as the imagination synthesizes it serves the understanding, but in that role it also brings to bear some of its own formative power. We have seen *Bildung* at work before in empirical processes of image formation, but here it is displayed in the production of schemata.

Schemata are a priori products of the imagination that mediate between concepts and empirical appearances. A schema, according to Kant, "must be pure, that is, void of all empirical content, and yet at the same time, while it must in one respect be *intellectual*, it must in another be *sensible*" (*CI*, A138/B177).

Most discussions of the schematism focus on the schemata of the *pure* concepts of the understanding. These are the transcendental schemata that apply the categories to make them constitutive of our experience of empirical objects. The task of the imagination is to mediate between the conceptual universality of the categories and the empirical particularity of sensible intuition. It does so by applying the categories to the most universal condition of sense, namely, the form of time. The imagination schematizes by translating the rules implicit in the categories into a temporally ordered set of instructions for constructing an objectively determinate nature. The category of causality, for example, provides the rule for recognizing a temporal order as a necessary order. This can be schematized by the imagination as a progressive temporal sequence through which objects can be determinately related. The production of temporal schemata can be seen to constitute the basic synthetical transcendental function of the imagination.

Kant also speaks of schemata of *pure sensible* concepts, which must be discriminated from the above schemata of the pure concepts of the understanding. Whereas the schema of a pure concept of the understanding "can never be brought into any image whatsoever," the schema of a pure sensible concept is one "through which, and in accordance with which, images themselves first become possible" (*CI*, A142/B181). The schema of a pure sensible concept, such as of a figure in space, is not to be confused with an image of an empirical concept.[5] The reproductive imagination, as an empirical faculty, involved images, but here the imagination produces schemata that make images possible, but that cannot themselves be images or be drawn from images. "No image could ever be adequate to the concept of a triangle in general," Kant writes. "The schema of the triangle can exist nowhere but in thought. It is a rule of synthesis of the imagination, in respect to pure figures in space" (*C1*, A141/B180).

In keeping with the theme of a figurative or figure-producing imagination, Kant calls the schema of a pure sensible concept a "monogram" (*C1*, A142/B181). Later, at A570/B598, Kant describes a monogram as "a sketch or outline that hovers in the midst of various experiences," one that is treated as a "shadowy image (*Schattenbild*)" (III, 385). Because this description is being used to create a contrast with an ideal of reason, there is the unfortunate suggestion that a monogram is a vague empirical image. But, clearly, as a schema a monogram cannot be empirical and must be understood as a rule for generating configurations of lines.

It is interesting to note that Kant refers to space when speaking of a monogram of pure a priori imagination and to time when speaking of the transcendental schema of the categories. The categories are schematized primarily in terms of time, which, as the form of inner sense, is more inclusive than space, the form of outer sense. However, in the B Deduction the idea of a "figurative synthesis" suggests that the schemata of pure intellectual concepts, which were first conceived purely in terms of time, may also incorporate some of the spatial qualities associated with the schemata of pure sensible concepts. At B154, Kant identifies the figurative synthesis as a "determination of the manifold by the transcendental act of imagination (synthetic influence of the understanding upon inner sense)." In illustrating this influence on inner sense, Kant writes that the drawing of a straight line serves "as the outer figurative representation of time" (*C1*, B154). With this last reference he brings a spatial dimension into the temporal form of inner sense.

The fact that in the new Deduction and the Refutation of Idealism

---

5. An empirical concept does not have its own schema, but "always stands in immediate relation to the schema of . . . some specific universal concept" (*C1*, A141/B180), i.e., in applying the latter (see chapter 3).

of the B edition Kant makes space the condition for the determination of time is significant for the possibility of relating these temporal and spatial schemata. Inner sense may be more inclusive than outer sense because it can incorporate all the contents of the latter, but it derives its determination from its relation to objects of outer sense. Even the concept of succession, which in the A edition seemed a primitive temporal concept, turns out in the B edition to be inseparable from space. Kant writes, "Motion, as an act of the subject (not as a determination of an object), and therefore the synthesis of the manifold in space, first produces the concept of succession" (*C1*, B154–55). Succession as a feature of inner sense must be derived from a motion of the imagination generating space-time. Moreover, any determination of inner sense presupposes something permanent in outer sense.

It would be wrong to conclude, however, that the B edition makes time as such dependent on space. If anything their relationship is conceived as reciprocal, as can be illustrated by the schematization of the relational categories of substance, cause, and reciprocal action in terms of time as duration, succession, and coexistence. Given that all representations in inner sense are successive, spatial coexistence cannot be experienced without the category of reciprocal action. Thus for Kant the concept of reciprocally related substances in time is necessary for space to become fully objective, i.e., the space of simultaneously coexisting substances.[6]

The idea of a figurative synthesis suggests a greater affinity between the spatial and temporal schemata as well as the convergence of processes of synthesis and formation in the production of monogrammatic schemata. The monogram, understood as a rule for generating spatial forms, can be regarded as the transcendental condition for the synoptic image formation by which several perspectives are incorporated into one present-oriented *Abbild*.

Up to this point, monograms produced by the imagination have been discussed as schemata for mathematical figures. However, in its most common usage a monogram is a configuration of letters or initials that stands for a name. Similarly, the figurative synthesis of imagination can be explicated in linguistic as well as mathematical terms.

6. For more on the problem of simultaneity see chapter 4.

Experience as a "Reading" of Nature

In the *Critique of Pure Reason* and the *Prolegomena to Any Future Metaphysics* Kant indicates that the task of understanding is to give a reading of nature. In the latter work he writes that if "the pure concepts of the understanding are thought to go beyond objects of experience to things in themselves (*noumena*), they have no meaning whatever. They serve, as it were, only to spell out appearances, that we may be able to read them as experience."[7] The concepts of the understanding acquire their objective meaning through the figurative synthesis which applies them to sense impressions. The spelling-reading metaphor can be used to show that the imagination plays a crucial role in relating the categories to the objects of experience.

If a monogrammatic schema of a pure sensible concept enables us to discern recurrent mathematical patterns in sense, then a transcendental schema of a pure intellectual concept indicates what kind of meaning can be predicated of objects of experience. When dealing with letters, the former deciphers them as alphabetical characters,[8] while the latter reads them as words. In fact, we can distinguish four activities that Kant associates with language and the analysis of textual material, namely, spelling (*buchstabieren*), deciphering (*entziffern*), reading (*lesen*), and interpreting (*auslegen*).[9] Normally, one reads letters as spelling out words that have meaning, but if the letters are illegible or scrambled, one must attempt to decipher them. On the other hand, if there is a problem on the level of the meaning of words or sentences, then one must appeal to interpretation.

In his *Erscheinung bei Kant* (Appearance in Kant) Gerold Prauss also appeals to Kant's reading metaphor as part of an attempt to clarify the distinction between judgments of perception and judgments

7. Kant, *Prolegomena to Any Future Metaphysics* (hereafter *PFM*), trans. G. Carus and L. W. Beck (Indianapolis: Bobbs-Merrill, 1950), 60; IV, 312.

8. It should be noted that the term Kant uses for algebra in *Buchstabenrechnung* (calculation by means of letters) (*C1*, A717/B745).

9. These four terms can be found in a variety of Kant's writings, but since the topic of language is not examined in any extended way, they provide mere working distinctions, which can in some cases be refined. Manfred Riedel writes that "language is for Kant one of those concepts of reason which are of immediate concern to the matter of critique and just because of that it never becomes *thematic*." See his *Urteilskraft und Vernunft: Kants ursprüngliche Fragestellung* (Frankfurt am Main: Suhrkamp, 1989), 49. Riedel considers Kant's concept of language "an *operative concept of reason*" (*Urteilskraft*, 49).

of experience. Whereas a judgment of experience is a full-fledged construal (*Deutung*) that applies the categories to a manifold, the judgment of perception merely uses the categories in some derivative sense. In effect they differ in giving strong and weak readings of the manifold of intuition. Prauss distinguishes ordinary reading from deciphering, which he describes as "a reading that must come to terms with its characters letter by letter."[10] But for the most part deciphering, reading, and interpreting are merged in his discussion of the process of construal (*Deutung*).[11]

The distinction between deciphering, reading, and interpreting can be correlated with three of the basic functions of the imagination that we have distinguished. Deciphering can be related to the formation of monogrammatic schemata; reading (whether of words or of the manifold of sense) involves the schematization of the categories; finally, interpretation, or *Auslegung,* calls upon the *Ausbildung,* or completing functions, of the imagination that we discussed in chapter 1 and shall examine more fully in chapter 6.

If the text to be construed is the so-called book of nature, the task of deciphering is to discover the basic mathematical patterns (*Urbilder*) that run through what is intuited. Those patterns that recur can be derived from monogrammatic schemata. In an essay published in 1764 Kant specifically speaks of deciphering in relation to mathematics. Mathematical signs or ciphers become independent of their original reference and can then be manipulated without any thought of their object. Yet what is learned through the manipulation of the ciphers also applies to the objects.[12] The mathematical cipher becomes an intuitive replacement of the object (it is called a "sign *in concreto*"), whereas philosophical language is restricted to words that can at best represent their objects abstractly (see II, 278–79).

To explicate what is involved in reading and interpreting nature as a

10. Gerold Prauss, *Erscheinung bei Kant: Ein Problem der "Kritik der reinen Vernunft"* (Berlin: Walter de Gruyter & Co., 1971), 205.

11. Although J. M. Young gives an excellent account of the imagination in Kant's *Critique of Pure Reason* by showing that it involves more than imaging, he too makes no distinction between construing and interpreting. He writes: "The characteristic act of imagination is thus to construe or interpret something perceived (e.g., the line on the chalkboard) as something other or more than what it is perceived as being (e.g., as a lever)." "Kant's View of Imagination," *Kant-Studien* 79 (1988): 142.

12. See Kant, *Untersuchung über die Deutlichkeit der Grundsätze der natürlichen Theologie und der Moral* (see chap. 1, n. 8); II, 278.

text, we must first examine the section "Ideas in General" in the Transcendental Dialectic of the *Critique of Pure Reason*. The opening discussion of ideas contains some interesting reflections on meaning and interpretation as Kant seeks to define his own use of the term "idea" in relation to Plato's.[13] According to Kant, Plato was wrong to conceive of ideas or forms as the archetypes (*Urbilder*) of things themselves, but he rightly "realised that our faculty of knowledge feels a much higher need than merely *to spell out* appearances according to a synthetic unity, in order to be able *to read* them as experience. He knew that our reason naturally exalts itself to modes of knowledge which . . . transcend the bounds of experience" (*C1*, A314/B370–71; emphases added). In this passage, Kant's language suggests a way to reformulate the differing goals of the understanding and reason as the difference between reading and interpreting. The goal of the understanding is to "read" as experience what is spelled out according to concepts in the manifold of appearances. But reason seeks more. It seeks to interpret these experiences in terms of an idea of a whole. If concepts of the understanding provide the *rules for reading* the manifold of sense so as to produce knowledge of objects in nature, then ideas of reason can be said to provide the *rules for interpreting* these objects so as to form a coherent and complete system of nature.

A relation between the ideas of reason and an interpretation of the system of nature is actually suggested in a *Reflexion zur Metaphysik* where Kant warns that ideas of reason may not be used dogmatically to explain nature by means of causes that transcend nature. Such ideas of reason can only be used regulatively, "for nature is our task, the text of our interpretation."[14] The notion of interpreting nature is most fully explored in the *Opus postumum*, where Kant discusses the systematization of fundamental forces and of the laws of nature. He distinguishes two kinds of "interpretation (*Auslegung*) of nature."[15] The first kind is a "doctrinal (*doktrinale*)" interpretation that he retrospectively attributes to the *Metaphysical Foundations of Natural Science* (see *OP*, XXII, 173): in that work Kant had interpreted substance as matter that is movable in space and subject to motion in time (see *OP*, XXII, 189). The second kind of interpretation is called "authentic (*au-*

13. For a more detailed analysis of these reflections on interpretation see chapter 8.
14. Kant, *Reflexionen zur Metaphysik* (hereafter *RM*), (see chap. 1, n. 8), no. 5637; XVIII, 274 (1780–83).
15. Kant, *Opus postumum* (hereafter *OP*) (see chap. 1, n. 8), XXII, 173.

thentisch)" and will be provided by the science of physics when it works out the actual laws of nature (see *OP*, XXII, 173).

Kant does not tell us explicitly what the distinction between doctrinal and authentic interpretations signifies.[16] He calls the doctrinal interpretation of the *Metaphysical Foundations of Natural Science* "a scholastic system (*Lehrsystem*)" (*OP*, XXII, 189), in contrast to the "experiential system (*Erfahrungssystem*)" of physics (*OP*, XXII, 173). In the Canon of Pure Reason of the first *Critique* Kant applies the term "doctrinal" to belief rather than interpretation. He places doctrinal beliefs between contingent pragmatic beliefs and absolute moral beliefs (*CI*, A825/B853–A828/B856). A doctrinal belief is strongly held as "hypothetically necessary" (*CI*, A823/B851) for the attainment of some theoretical end. It falls short of a moral belief, which is characterized as "absolutely necessary" (*CI*, A828/B856). This suggests that the doctrinal interpretation or scholastic system of the *Metaphysical Foundations of Natural Science* provides a systematization of nature that is still hypothetical or speculative. The authentic interpretation of nature aimed at by physics would be nonspeculative in that it goes back to the original sources of experience and is purely law-derived.

The *Metaphysical Foundations of Natural Science* appeals to two original forces of repulsion and attraction, but of these only repulsion is directly related to experience. The repulsive force manifests itself in the extension, impenetrability, and resistance of bodies. Attraction, by contrast, can only be inferred because in itself it "can give us either no sensation at all or at least no determinate object of sensation."[17] It must be posited as a counter to the repulsive force, which by itself would lead to the infinite dispersal of matter. Although Kant considers attraction absolutely necessary for explaining the properties of physical reality, it is nevertheless a speculative, hypothetical force. The *Metaphysical Foundations of Natural Science* can thus provide only a doctrinal interpretation. According to the *Opus postumum,* physics itself must give an authentic interpretation of reality which system-

16. Although the term "doctrinal" occurs throughout Kant's corpus, the phrase "authentic interpretation" is used primarily when he considers issues in religious hermeneutics and may have been appropriated from Georg Friedrich Meier, *Versuch einer allgemeinen Auslegungskunst* (Halle: Carl Hermann Hemmerde, 1757); reprint ed. by L. Geldsetzer (Düsseldorf: Stern-Verlag Janssen & Co., 1965), §136–138. I am grateful to Jean Grondin for this reference.

17. Kant, *Metaphysical Foundations of Natural Science* (hereafter *MFNS*), trans. James Ellington (Indianapolis: Bobbs-Merrill, 1970), 59.

atizes our experience of reality purely on the basis of the laws of nature.[18]

In contrast to these works, the *Critique of Pure Reason* is directed more to the *reading* of nature *as experience* than to its interpretation as a system. It gives a conventional and linear reading of the manifold of sense in terms of the objects of possible experience. The distinction between reading and interpretation is appropriate because in the one case we begin with units of meaning, in the other with an integrated total meaning. Reading is first of all a linear process of combining letters into the unit-meanings of words and constructing the meaning of sentences from those words. This corresponds with what Kant says about the discursive nature of the understanding and its efforts to construct the objects of experience. There is an obvious parallel between the process of reading lines of letters and the process of ordering the impressions of sense into the linear temporal form of inner sense. In both cases we proceed from part to whole. But interpretation can begin only when we have some sense of a whole, just as system-building requires ideas of reason that consider our already existing experiences of objects holistically.

The problem of drawing a line in thought, which was raised in relation to the syntheses of apprehending, reproducing, and recognizing the unity of a manifold in inner sense, can now be reconsidered in light of the reading metaphor. Kant's suggestion in the Subjective Deduction that we imagine a line part by part seemed artificial, for we usually grasp it at a glance. But if drawing a temporal line in inner sense involves reading a manifold, then Kant's part by part approach makes more sense. We do compose sentences word by word; we do arrange words in lines; and we do read these lines from left to right. The possibility of the first parts of a line dropping out of thought as we move to the last parts is a real one if the line is like a line of prose. In reading sentences of any complexity we always stand in danger of losing sight of the opening words without an ongoing reproductive synthesis of the imagination. This is not the reproductive synthesis that Kant later dismissed as belonging to empirical psychology. In the Subjective Deduction Kant also spoke of imaginative reproduction as necessary for attaining a complete representation. The reproduc-

18. See chapter 7 for a more extended discussion of the distinction between doctrinal and authentic interpretation. Both biblical exegesis and the interpretation of history must be authenticated by the moral law.

tion involved in this process is a reproduction of what has just been produced and need not appeal to past experiential associations, which would differ for every subject. Without this direct mode of reproduction "a complete representation would never be obtained: . . . not even the present and most elementary representations of space and time" (*C1*, A102). What is discussed in the Subjective Deduction as necessary for the construction of mathematical lines and numbers also plays a central role in the linear reading of the manifold of inner sense.

With a mathematical or alphabetical monogram a given manifold of sense is deciphered in terms of a set of conventional forms or letters that are not tied to the subjective limits of empirical association. One of Kant's main ways of distinguishing epistemology from psychology was to conceive of the contents of consciousness in terms of formal mathematical relations that are constitutive of intersubjective experience. The reading metaphor can be used to extend this formal analysis of consciousness by adding a conventional linguistic dimension to epistemology. In this context the imagination can assume a quasi-linguistic role.

The synthesis of apprehension can be seen in both the process of reading letters as words and that of reading words for their place in the meaning of a sentence. In both cases we apprehend a linear sequence by quickly running its constituents together—much like Kant's description of the synthesis of apprehension as "running through" and "gathering together" the manifold. Finally, the synthesis of recognition can be said to operate on every level, that of the unit-meaning of the word, the sentence, the paragraph, etc.

The comparison with reading may help to account for both the cumulative and presuppositional character of the three syntheses in the Subjective Deduction. We saw at the beginning of this chapter that although the three forms of synthesis are developed "starting from below," the last is already presupposed by the first. This circularity makes better sense in terms of the reading process. If apprehending a manifold is at the same time a process of reading it as experience, then the circular relation that exists between the meaning of particular words and the meaning of the sentence of which they are parts cannot be ignored. It is the meaning of the sentence as a whole that determines which of the possible senses of a word are appropriate. Thus the sentence is not merely the aggregation of the particular words that constitute it. Its projected unity establishes the meaning of these words. On the level of the sentence, the synthesis of apprehension can be said to run through the particular words to project an indeterminate whole, which is then determined by the more deliberate syntheses of reproduction and recognition. The crucial added dimension introduced by the metaphor of reading is that of meaning. To apprehend letters as words is at the same time to recognize their meaning. Similarly, to read what is spelled out in the manifold of sense as experience is to recognize the meaning of what is apprehended.

Schematism and Objective Meaning

The chapter on the schematism shows that the imagination is necessary if the categories are to receive an objective meaning. As Kant writes at the conclusion of this chapter: "The categories . . . without schemata, are merely functions of the understanding for concepts; and represent no object. This [objective] meaning (*Bedeutung*) they acquire from sensibility, which realises the understanding in the very process of restricting it" (*C1*, A147/B187; III, 139). Prior to being schematized by the imagination, the categories are empty, or have only a logical meaning. Their objective meaning requires the contribution of the imagination. The significance of this contribution of the imagination becomes especially clear in the B Deduction.

The move from logical to objective meaning is signaled by a change in Kant's use of different German terms for "object." Early in the B Deduction, Kant defines the transcendental unity of apperception as "that unity through which all the manifold in an intuition is united in a concept of the object (*Objekt*)" (*C1*, B139; III, 113). Subsequently when referring to the objective meaning of the categories Kant speaks of *Gegenstand* instead of *Objekt*. The categories must be related "to objects (*Gegenstände*) of intuition in general, whether that intuition be our own or any other, provided only it be sensible" (*C1*, B150; III, 119).

Henry Allison, among others, has recently pointed to the importance of the distinction between *Objekt* and *Gegenstand*.[19] In his view, there are two main concerns of the B Deduction: first to prove the

19. Henry Allison, *Kant's Transcendental Idealism* (New Haven: Yale University Press, 1983), 135–36, 158–61. For an examination of the distinction in the A edition, see Charles Sherover, "Two Kinds of Transcendental Objectivity: Their Differentiation," in *Essays on Kant's "Critique of Pure Reason,"* ed. J. N. Mohanty and Robert Shahan (Norman: University of Oklahoma Press, 1982), 251–78.

objective validity of the categories, and second to show their objective reality as well. "Objective validity," he writes, "goes together with a judgmental or logical conception of an object (*Objekt*)" whereas "objective reality is connected with a 'real' sense of object (*Gegenstand*)."[20] According to Allison's step by step account of the B Deduction, Kant does not actually connect the categories to the *Gegenstand* of human sensibility until §26, where he introduces the synthesis of apprehension, which deals with real objects. This is because the transcendental synthesis discussed in §24 is interpreted to apply only to "the forms of human sensibility," while the synthesis of apprehension applies to the "empirical content" of human sensibility.[21]

Allison's analysis is directed to the question of objective *reality*, but an alternative interpretation can be proposed from the point of view of the imagination's contribution to objective *meaning*. In discussing figurative synthesis Kant defines the imagination as "the faculty of representing in intuition an object (*Gegenstand*) even (*auch*) *without its presence*" (*CI*, B151; III, 119–20). Because the object of the imagination need not be present, one could say that it is merely projected; but the important thing is that it is projected as a *Gegenstand*. The imagination makes possible the crucial transition from logical meaning to objective meaning. Here at §24 the understanding is already referred "to the *Gegenstände* of our possible intuitions" (*CI*, B152; III, 120), not just to the forms of our intuition. In §26 Kant merely specifies the claims of §24 by showing that the categories must apply to "everything that can be presented to our senses" (*CI*, B160). On this reading the synthesis of apprehension is subsumable under the transcendental synthesis of the imagination.

The contrast between *Objekt* and *Gegenstand* is not only that between logical and real objects. Kant also speaks of an "*Objekt* distinct from me" (*CI*, B158) and of "an *Objekt* of intuition" (*CI*, B156). This indicates that an *Objekt* need not be merely logical; it can be just as real as a *Gegenstand*. On the one extreme, the term *Objekt* is referred to a pure logical object, and on the other extreme, to whatever is given to me as mere material. For example, the understanding is said to arrange "the material of knowledge, that is, the intuition which must be

20. Allison, *Idealism*, 135.
21. Allison, *Idealism*, 163, 175.

given to it by the *Objekt*" (*C1*, B145; III, 116). Thus anything either merely thought or merely sensed would be an *Objekt* and becomes a *Gegenstand*—an object of experience—only through the mediation of the imagination. The difference between *Objekt* and *Gegenstand* is between an unmediated object and an object mediated by the schemata of the imagination.

The Deduction having shown *that* the categories apply to all perceptual experience, the Schematism chapter shows *in what way* they apply. In terms of the reading of nature, the schemata may be considered as semantical rules that determine the conformity of the *Gegenstand* to the categories by specifying its possible empirical predicates. As argued by Robert Butts, the categories can be considered syntactical and the schemata, semantical: "Categories are grammatical forms; to supply meanings that will take these forms something else is required, namely rules that tell us to what the forms shall be applied. . . . The schemata specify in general terms what kinds of observation predicates are permitted given the epistemic form of the system."[22] In accordance with Kant's conception of natural science, the semantical rules only admit predicates whose meaning can be determined in terms of the mathematically measurable.

By conceiving schemata as semantical rules we can better understand Kant's remark that the objective meaning made possible by the schemata both "realizes" and "restricts" the understanding (see the first paragraph of this section). The schemata realize the categorical forms by anticipating possible objects of experience while at the same time they restrict them by selecting what type of empirical concepts are eligible to be applied to such objects.

If the categories provide the grammatical rules whereby we order the manifold of sense in terms of certain basic formal patterns such as the subject-predicate relation, then the schemata of the imagination can be said to anticipate these patterns in terms of particular types of object-attribute relations. Whatever the sensuous manifold tells us about the object, the schemata teach us to select that which is measurable. Thus among the paragraphs of information recorded in the successive manifold of sense, only certain sentences need be focused on for their relevance to what is scientifically measurable. The sche-

22. Robert E. Butts, "Kant's Schemata as Semantical Rules," in *Kant Studies Today*, ed. Lewis W. Beck (La Salle, Ill.: Open Court, 1969), 294.

mata teach us to read selectively as the imagination singles out in advance some of the manifolds of sense that can be made scientifically meaningful.

Conclusion

Whereas in the first chapter we saw the imagination forming images, in this chapter we have focused on the two mediating functions of the imagination in Kant's epistemology, i.e., figurative synthesis and the anticipation of the meaning of objects made possible by schematization. We have seen Kant move from the image-producing model of the imagination to one where the syntheses of the imagination produce meaning by reading the manifold of sense as experience of objects in nature.

The imagination plays an important role in the constitution of objects of experience from the manifold of sense, and in this role the imagination becomes the handmaiden of the understanding. But in serving the needs of the understanding we have seen the imagination bring distinctive powers to bear in applying the categories to the manifold of sense. Its formative powers are still evident in the figurative synthesis and the production of monogrammatic schemata. Moreover, we have interpreted the space-time generating motion of the imagination as a linear process of reading that supplies the meaning of objects of experience. The fact that Kant concludes that all synthesis is a function of the understanding means only that the imagination is subservient to the understanding insofar as it synthesizes. This is important to keep in mind as we now turn to the *Critique of Judgment*.

Part Two

The Imagination in the
Critique of Judgment

3

The Aesthetic Imagination:
Beautiful Form and
Reflective Specification

In this part I shall examine the imagination in the *Critique of Judgment* (1790), where its role is extended in relation to reflective judgment. The imagination's tasks are no longer defined primarily in terms of their use for the objective determinant judgments of the understanding. This basic fact must be underscored at the outset, for many of the significant developments in Kant's theory of the imagination remain unrecognized in commentaries written from the standpoint of the agenda of the *Critique of Pure Reason*. While the transcendental foundation of the first *Critique* remains unchallenged, the shift from determinant to reflective judgment—from the conditions of ordinary and scientific experience to those of aesthetic consciousness—gives rise to an important redefinition and expansion of the imagination's tasks.

The major changes that occur in the *Critique of Judgment* will be investigated in their various aspects over the course of the next three chapters. The main focus in this chapter will be on the introductions and the Analytic of the Beautiful as they define the imagination in reflective judgment and in the judgment of taste or beauty. This will be followed by chapters relating the imagination to aesthetic judgments about the sublime (chapter 4) as well as to the life of the feelings in general (chapter 5).

The Imagination in Aesthetic Judgment

In the Analytic of the Beautiful, the imagination functions in accordance with the basic conditions established by Kant for judgments of beauty, or taste. As the purest type of aesthetic judgment, the judgment of taste fulfills the requirements set forth in the four moments of the Analytic: (1) it must be based on a "disinterested satisfaction";[1] (2) it must be universally valid without being derived from a concept (see *C3*, §8, 49); (3) it may have "nothing at its basis but the form of the purposiveness of an object" (*C3*, §11, 56), i.e., it involves a subjective purposiveness that does not attribute any purpose to its object; finally, (4) it should demand from others an agreement that is subjectively necessary (*C3*, §19, 74).

The judgment of taste can be contrasted on the one hand with empirical aesthetic judgments about the pleasantness of the content of our representations and on the other hand with intellectual aesthetic judgments by which we judge the beauty of "objects which come under the concept of a particular purpose" (*C3*, §16, 65). These other kinds of aesthetic judgments do not display the disinterested pleasure of the judgment of taste: empirical aesthetic judgments are based on a sensuous interest and intellectual aesthetic judgments on interest in perfection, or in what an object ought to be.[2] Unless otherwise noted, when I speak of aesthetic judgment in this chapter I will be referring to the pure aesthetic judgment that Kant calls the judgment of taste.

The activity of the imagination in aesthetic judgments is characterized by what Kant calls a "lively play" (*C3*, §9, 54). In addition to being productive, the imagination is described as spontaneous, literally "self-activating (*selbsttätig*)," and as "the author of voluntary (*willkürlicher*) forms of possible intuitions" (*C3*, §22, 77; V, 240). In the *Critique of Pure Reason* the figurative syntheses of the imagination were restricted by the aims of definite objective cognition and strictly bound by the laws of the understanding. The aesthetic imagination, being productive and self-activating, is freer than that. It can play with possible forms, but its play does not exhibit unlimited freedom, because in the apprehension of beautiful objects the imagination "is tied to a definite form" (*C3*, §22, 78). The peculiar pleasure we find in judging an object to be beautiful lies in "the imagination's *free conformity to law*" (*C3*, §22, 77). Although self-activating, the aesthetic imagination is not autonomous, that is, it does not establish its own

---

1. Kant, *Critique of Judgment* (hereafter *C3*), trans. J. H. Bernard (New York: Hafner Press, 1974), §6, 45.

2. The imagination's role in empirical aesthetic judgments is merely pathological and will be of only marginal interest. Intellectual aesthetic judgments are central to the appreciation of art and will require a consideration of the relation between the creative imagination and aesthetic ideas (see chapter 6).

laws. It conforms to laws that are still the laws of the understanding. The "free conformity" of the aesthetic imagination to the laws of the understanding means that the imagination may not violate the categorial framework of the understanding, although it may explicate possibilities left open by that framework.

In aesthetic consciousness the relation between imagination and understanding is one of "subjective agreement" (*C3*, §22, 78) manifested as aesthetic pleasure. This is contrasted with the "objective agreement" in the normal judgment of experience, where a representation "is referred to a definite concept of an object" (*C3*, §22, 78) and the imagination serves the understanding by subsuming representations of sense to concepts. The subjective agreement between the imagination and the understanding in an aesthetic judgment is not based on subordination of one to the other, but involves the free coordination and the mutual play of the two faculties.

This aesthetic relation, which Kant calls a harmony, is commonly held to be a synthesis. A. H. Trebels writes: "The subjective agreement of the free play of the imagination with the free lawfulness of the understanding is to be regarded as a synthesis."[3] Peter Heintel characterizes beauty as an "open synthesis" between the subject and the object.[4] And in an earlier work I have also spoken of a "vague synthesis of harmony, not strong enough to bind the contents of sense presented by the work of art, but sufficient to refer the forms of representations to our feeling."[5] However, I now think that it is misleading to call a felt harmony between the imagination and the understanding a synthesis. A harmony involves a reciprocal relation between two distinct elements; a synthesis, as Kant conceives it, involves a one-sided influence for the sake of a strict unity. In the syntheses of the first *Critique* concepts are imposed on sense, and Kant speaks of "the synthetic influence of the understanding upon inner sense" (*C1*, B154). Thus to consider the play of the two faculties in aesthetic harmony a synthesis is to endanger the freedom of conformity to law

---

3. Andreas Heinrich Trebels, *Einbildungskraft und Spiel; Untersuchungen zur Kantischen Ästhetik* (*Kantstudien Ergänzungsheft* 93 [Bonn: H. Bouvier u. Co. Verlag, 1967], 119). Trebels also claims that play is the medium of aesthetic synthesis (207).

4. Peter Heintel, *Die Bedeutung der Kritik der ästhetischen Urteilskraft für die transzendentale Systematik* (*Kantstudien Ergänzungsheft* 99 [Bonn: H. Bouvier u. Co. Verlag, 1970], 42).

5. Rudolf A. Makkreel, *Dilthey, Philosopher of the Human Studies* (Princeton: Princeton University Press, 1975), 187.

attributed to the imagination. Moreover, analysis of the aesthetic functions of the imagination will show that the general assumption of the continued importance of synthesis in the third *Critique* must be questioned.

Synthesis and Aesthetic Apprehension

The fact that Kant makes no use of the term "synthesis" in discussing the imagination's role in aesthetic apprehension and aesthetic comprehension[6] has remained largely unnoticed, although this stands in marked contrast to the *Critique of Pure Reason*, where all the functions of the imagination—whether concerning the apprehension of space, the reproduction of images, or the production of schemata—are described in terms of acts of synthesis. It could, of course, be argued that the lack of reference to synthesis merely means that Kant does not wish to repeat his well-known claims and belabor the obvious; but this interpretation is not convincing, for Kant never hesitates to restate his main positions wherever they apply. To understand why specific acts of imaginative synthesis are omitted from Kant's discussion of beauty, we must look to the conditions of aesthetic consciousness and reflective judgment.

When Kant speaks of aesthetic judgments as synthetic, he is only claiming that they are synthetic in form. "Judgments of taste are synthetical," Kant asserts, "because they go beyond the concept and even beyond the intuition of the object (*Objekt*), and add to that intuition as predicate something that is not a cognition, viz., a feeling of pleasure (or pain)" (*C3*, §36, 131). They are not synthetic in the objective sense applicable to cognitive judgments, in which we add to the concept of an object a concept of one of its attributes. Instead of claiming something about the objective properties of an object, the judgment of taste discloses something about our own subjective state of mind in apprehending the form of an object.

Insofar as the content of the subject-term is amplified, aesthetic judgments may be considered synthetic in form. However, when I say "This rose is beautiful" the amplification obviously differs from that contained in the proposition "This rose is red." The latter can be said to involve the synthesis of two empirical concepts. By contrast, the

6. Aesthetic comprehension will be dealt with in the next chapter, on the sublime.

predicate "beautiful" adds to my apprehension of the rose merely the consciousness that I feel pleasure about it. Beauty is not something that can be connected to the rose as one of its qualities. There is no act of synthesis that expands the concept of a rose. Nor can the apprehension of the rose and the pleasure be merged. The former is directed at the object, the latter at the subject. Those two divergent directions of attention cannot be strictly unified by a synthesis. They can at best be harmonized.

In the *Logic* Kant states that synthesis involves a "making distinct of objects."[7] On this score, the judgment of taste is synthetic only in an attenuated sense, for the added feeling of pleasure does not serve to make its object more distinct. The judgment of taste is also synthetic in the general sense that it is subject to the basic condition established in the first *Critique* for the consciousness of objects, namely, the synthetic unity of apperception. What further transcendental conditions established in the first *Critique* are operative in aesthetic consciousness will be examined in the next section, which concerns the presentation of concepts in reflective judgment. The point to be made here is that the extent to which the conditions of the first *Critique* can be transferred to the third *Critique* is limited by the different functions assigned to the imagination in its aesthetic setting.

Since the aesthetic judgment does not establish a determinate, objective synthesis, it may be thought to be based on a synthesis that is subjective. On this view aesthetic apprehension is seen as a subjective preconceptual synthesis of the imagination. At first glance, such an interpretation of aesthetic apprehension appears to be supported by a key passage in which Kant claims that aesthetic pleasure involves "the mere apprehension (*apprehensio*) of the form of an object of intuition without reference to a concept for a definite cognition" (*C3*, intro., vii, 26). Thus in Paul Guyer's account of the harmony of the faculties, the contributions of the imagination are described in terms of the preconceptual syntheses of apprehension and reproduction of the Subjective Deduction of the first *Critique*.[8] These syntheses without concepts, which were later rejected by Kant as having no place within the critical framework, are now revived by Guyer in a psychological

7. Kant, *Logic: A Manual for Lectures* (hereafter *L*), trans. Robert S. Hartman and Wolfgang Schwarz (Indianapolis: Bobbs-Merrill, 1974), 70.

8. Paul Guyer, *Kant and the Claims of Taste* (Cambridge: Harvard University Press, 1979), 86.

sense. They are construed as subjective activities that provide a preparatory synthesis of the manifold of intuition that must harmonize with a final conceptual synthesis of the understanding. The activities of the aesthetic imagination are treated as part of "the psychological concomitants of knowledge."[9] Such a psychological defense of syntheses without concepts places aesthetic harmony outside the transcendental discourse of the *Critique of Judgment* and makes it appear that Kant has gone back on the important result of the first *Critique* that all syntheses are dependent on concepts of the understanding.

It should be noted, however, that in his discussion of taste Kant is speaking of an apprehension without concepts, not a synthesis without concepts. His text supplies no direct evidence for equating the aesthetic apprehension of imagination with the *syntheses* of apprehension and reproduction, for there is no mention of synthesis in his account of aesthetic apprehension without a concept. The synthesis of apprehension of the Subjective Deduction was an elementary process of intuiting the manifold of sense and therefore cannot be identified with the aesthetic apprehension of form by the imagination. As for the syntheses of reproduction, Kant's explicit statement that the imagination is *not* reproductive in the judgment of taste (see C3, §22, 77) indicates that it should be excluded from aesthetic apprehension.

Kant's claim that the aesthetic imagination is not reproductive may appear problematic, for, as Donald Crawford writes, " 'experience as such necessarily presupposes the reproducibility of appearances' (A102), and the experience of an object of art would seem to be no exception."[10] This would present a difficulty if Kant were in fact describing the "experience" of art objects rather than the "apprehension" of their form. The synthesis of reproduction is necessary only if we assume that all the sensible conditions established for experience in the *Critique of Pure Reason* also apply to aesthetic apprehension. In the construction of ordinary and scientific experience, the manifold of sense is synthesized into determinately unified objects whose states can be placed into relations of causal dependence. One of the conditions of this construction is that the manifold is represented

9. Guyer, *Claims of Taste*, 98.
10. Donald W. Crawford, *Kant's Aesthetic Theory* (Madison: University of Wisconsin Press, 1974), 90.

in inner sense as a temporal succession of discrete contents. We saw that each representation in inner sense disappears to make room for the next representation.[11] In order to be revived it must be reproduced by a subsequent act of the imagination and then recognized as the same representation. The synthesis of reproduction involved in the construction of objects of experience thus also requires a synthesis of recognition by means of an empirical concept.[12]

If the aesthetically apprehended form of an art object were a complete representation of this type, then apprehension of form would also require the syntheses of reproduction and recognition. But aesthetic apprehension is not an experience of a determinately constructed complex. Because an aesthetic form is a whole whose parts are not discretely sensed but felt to be an indeterminate unity, there is no need for special acts of empirical synthesis, whether of apprehension, reproduction, or recognition.

The Reflective Specification of the Categories

Since the cognitive tasks of the imagination were defined in terms of its syntheses, their absence in the *Critique of Judgment* may be mistaken to mean that the aesthetic imagination has no epistemological significance. This would reinforce the widespread view that Kant's aesthetic judgments, being based on feeling, have no cognitive import. To assume the continuing role of synthesis in the third *Critique* is one way to maintain the relevance of aesthetics for epistemological questions. Yet the result has been to place the aesthetic imagination in a precognitive sphere, contributing, in effect, an unconsummated or inferior mode of knowledge.

While Kant himself seems to withdraw aesthetic apprehension from the sphere of knowledge by saying that it occurs without a concept for a definite cognition, this means no more than that aesthetic judgments do not add to our stock of empirical knowledge. Although

11. Kant was most explicit about the successive form of inner sense in the Subjective Deduction of the *Critique of Pure Reason*, but it is apparent as well in the following statement, which he preserved in the B edition: "The apprehension of the manifold of appearance is always successive. The representations of the parts follow upon one another" (*C1*, A189/B234).

12. In chapter 5 we will see that aesthetic states can reproduce themselves without the syntheses of reproduction necessary to revive cognitive representations.

the aesthetic imagination does not serve the interest of determinant judgment in definite cognition of objects, it is a function of reflective judgment that has a bearing on the theoretical task of the systematization of experience. The judgment of taste is not directly cognitive, but nevertheless relates to "cognition in general" (*C3*, §12, 58).[13] The nonsynthetic functions of the imagination developed in relation to aesthetic consciousness and reflective judgment disclose unexpected cognitive implications.

The fact that aesthetic apprehension occurs without concepts does not entail that it stands in no relation to any at all. The one kind of concept that is specifically dispensed with is the empirical concept, for only such a concept would suffice for a definite cognition of the object. The situation is less clear in the case of categorial concepts. I have already claimed that the synthetic unity of apperception is a condition for both aesthetic and cognitive judgments. Mary Gregor has argued that since the categories are the rules whereby the synthetic unity of apperception is related to the manifold of sense, they must also be applicable to aesthetic apprehension even if the latter leaves the manifold an indeterminate "this." She writes, "In reflecting on the form of the object we are relating elements—lines, tones—to each other and ultimately to the unity of the representation 'this,' which is clearly a product of human consciousness and involves the categories."[14] Gregor's main concern is to show the applicability of the categories of quantity to judgments of taste. The applicability of the mathematical categories mainly entails that the object judged is measurable. It does not actually provide a mathematical determination that would amount to a cognition of the aesthetic object.

Lewis White Beck has also argued that the mathematical categories apply to judgments of taste. Focusing on the qualitative mathematical categories, he claims that they "certainly do apply to the qualities we experience aesthetically."[15] Aesthetic judgments are comparable to perceptual judgments such as "the sun looks bright" and "the stone feels warm." Even if such judgments were reformulated to omit all ref-

13. What the phrase "cognition in general" means will be explained in the last section of this chapter.

14. Mary Gregor, "Aesthetic Form and Sensory Content," in *The Philosophy of Immanuel Kant,* ed. Richard Kennington (Washington, D.C.: The Catholic University of America Press, 1985), 195.

15. Lewis White Beck, *Essays on Kant and Hume* (New Haven: Yale University Press, 1978), 56.

erence to objects—thereby excluding the dynamical category of substance—"the mathematical categories would still apply to the intensive magnitude of the brightness I see when I look at the sun and of the warmth I feel when I touch the stone."[16] Beck's position is that only the mathematical categories are involved in aesthetic judgments. The dynamical categories, such as the concepts of substance, causality, and reciprocity, are held to be inapplicable.[17] Since the dynamical categories were said in the first *Critique* to "bring the *existence* of appearances under rules *a priori*" (*C1*, A179/B221–2), they are thought to not apply to pure aesthetic judgments, which abstract from any interest in the existence of objects.

It should be noted, however, that Kant himself uses the dynamical category of causality when he attributes an "inner causality to aesthetic pleasure" (*C3*, §12, 58). To be sure, in so relating the category of causality to aesthetic judgment, Kant has said nothing about the causality of any object. The inner causality of aesthetic pleasure attaches merely to a state of mind of the subject. Here a category is used to unify, not the manifold of sense, but a state of mind. The inner causality of aesthetic pleasure is "purposive with respect of cognition in general" (*C3*, §12, 58).

I will argue in what follows that all the categories remain relevant to aesthetic judgments, but that they are used differently than in cognitive judgments. This difference can be brought out by noting how the role of the imagination changes in relation to reflective judgment. In the *Critique of Judgment* the categories are not used to synthesize the manifold of sense and to produce knowledge of objects. Instead, the imagination will be shown to specify the categories reflectively to organize pure mental contents.

Before we can explicate this new reflective function of the imagination, we must consider the way in which Kant contrasts determinant and reflective judgments in the two introductions to the *Critique of Judgment* and in his *Logic*. The introduction appearing with the *Critique of Judgment* itself is a second, shorter version of the original introduction, which was posthumously published (in 1922) with the title *First Introduction to the Critique of Judgment*. In a letter to Jakob Sigismund Beck, Kant explained that he had withheld the *First Intro-*

16. Beck, *Kant and Hume*, 52.
17. Beck, *Kant and Hume*, 52.

duction only because of its excessive length, and recommended it as "containing much that will contribute to a more complete insight into the concept of a teleology of nature."[18] Since the *First Introduction* makes many more detailed contrasts between determinant and reflective judgment, it is important for understanding the overall, reflective approach of the third *Critique*.

"Judgment in general," according to Kant, "is the faculty of thinking the particular as contained under the universal" (*C3*, intro., iv, 15). A determinant judgment is one in which the universal is given and the particular is to be found. In making a reflective judgment we must find a universal for a given particular. The latter may appear to be like an inductive judgment, but Kant is in fact speaking of a reflective power or faculty of judging (*reflektierende Urteilskraft*), which, according to his *Logic*, produces conclusions either by induction or by analogy (*L*, 136). Induction appeals to a "principle of generalization: What appertains to many things of a genus, that appertains to the remainder" (*L*, 136). Analogy appeals to a different principle—that of imaginative specification. It argues from the partial similarity of things in the same genus to total similarity according to what Kant calls "the principle of specification" (*L*, 136).

In the context of the *Critique of Judgment*, reflective judgment points to a fundamental transcendental principle, one whose "function is to establish the unity of all empirical principles under higher ones" (*C3*, intro., iv, 16). Since the purpose of this transcendental principle is the systematic unification of all laws of nature under empirical principles, we might say that the principles of generalization through induction and specification through analogy presuppose a reflective principle of systematization. According to the principle of determinant judgment, all particular objects are alike insofar as they can be *subordinated* to universal categories. Reflective judgment points up differences among objects by classifying them into various genera that can be *coordinated* into a system.

The different conditions established by determinant and reflective judgment influence the way concepts are employed in the two *Critiques*. In the *Critique of Pure Reason*, the imagination played a key role in the process of subordination by schematizing the concepts of the

18. Cited in Wilhelm Dilthey, *Gesammelte Schriften* (Göttingen: Vandenhoeck & Ruprecht, 1921), vol. 4, 341.

understanding. Although we have come to associate schematization with the specific cognitive tasks assigned to the imagination in producing determinant judgments, Kant indicates at one point that the imagination's schematizing power is also operative in the reflective system of the third *Critique*. At §35, Kant states that the freedom of the aesthetic imagination in reflective judgment "consists in the fact that it schematizes without a concept" (*C3*, §35, 129). Since the accepted definition of schematization is so closely identified with the process of conceptual determination, to speak of schematizing without a concept appears to be self-contradictory. What Kant seems to be pointing to here is the imagination's basic function of mediating between sensibility and intellect. However, within the context of reflective judgment the imagination's mediating role takes the form of presentation and specification rather than of schematization.

In the *Critique of Judgment* the schematization of concepts of the understanding is placed under the more general heading of presentation (*Darstellung*). Presentation, which can be considered as a covering term for the different ways that the imagination relates sensibility to the intellect, also includes the artistic process of symbolization (see chapter 6) and what I will discuss momentarily as reflective specification.

By turning to the *First Introduction* we can contrast the ways in which determinant and reflective judgments present concepts. In a determinant judgment presentation is described as the last of three acts necessary for arriving at an adequate empirical concept of an object. They are: "(1) the apprehension (*Auffassung*) of the manifold of intuition; (2) the comprehension (*Zusammenfassung*), i.e., the synthetic unity of consciousness of this manifold in the concept of an object (*Objekt*) (*apperceptio comprehensiva*); (3) the presentation (*exhibitio*) in intuition of the object (*Gegenstand*) corresponding to this concept."[19] Although Kant does not explicitly refer to schematization in the third step, its presence is made evident by his use of the term *Gegenstand*. As we saw in chapter 2, a *Gegenstand* is a schematized *Objekt*. If the *Gegenstand* of the third step is the object of an empirical concept, then presentation involves not merely the schematization of the categories but also their application to a real object.

19. Kant, *First Introduction to the Critique of Judgment* (hereafter *FI*), trans. James Haden (Indianapolis: Bobbs-Merrill, 1965), 24; XX, 220.

Kant then proceeds to characterize presentation in a reflective judgment without any reference to the conceptual comprehension or synthesis provided in step 2 of the determinant judgment. Because reflection is comparative, we find that reflection on aesthetic form involves a direct comparison of apprehension and presentation. Kant describes the aesthetic judgment of reflection as follows: "If the form of a given object (*Objekt*) in empirical intuition is so constituted that the *apprehension* of the manifold of the object in the imagination accords (*übereinkommt*) with the *presentation* of a concept of the understanding (regardless of which concept), then in mere reflection understanding and imagination mutually harmonize for the furtherance of their business, and the object (*Gegenstand*) is perceived as purposive for the judgment alone" (*FI*, 25; XX, 220–1). The fact that presentation is referred to both a concept of the understanding and a *Gegenstand* indicates that presentation in reflective judgment involves schematization; but it does not include the application of an empirical concept for the purpose of obtaining determinate knowledge of an object. This kind of application is not possible because the concept of the understanding is left undetermined.

We are now in a position to explicate Kant's earlier claim by saying that the aesthetic imagination schematizes without using *empirical* concepts. The aesthetic judgment directly compares the apprehended form of an object with the way categories are generally schematized in relation to the form of time and it is this accord that is aesthetically pleasing. Although Kant speaks of a harmony of the understanding and the imagination, what is actually compared in the aesthetic imagination are two products of the imagination, i.e., a form apprehended by the imagination and schemata as temporal rules of the imagination.

In the previous chapter we spoke of schematization as a process of applying the categories in terms of a linear temporal sequence that relates the contents of inner sense. By reading these contents in terms of possible objects of experience the imagination can preselect those attributes that are scientifically meaningful. In such cases, schematization was described as a process of anticipating particular objects to be subsumed under a concept. Now, in the *First Introduction*, Kant speaks of "specification" (*FI*, 19) in relation to the imaginative presentation involved in reflective judgment. This reflective process is not "mechanical" (*FI*, 18) like application, but proceeds "*artistically*, according to the universal but at the same time indeterminate principle of a purposive, systematic ordering of nature" (*FI*, 18; XX, 214).

The ordering of nature in terms of a system could be conceived empirically as an inductive process that ascends from the particular to the universal, whereby the objects of experience are classified in terms of species that can be ordered under higher genera. But this "*classification* of the manifold" presupposes a "*specification* of the manifold" that "begins with the universal concept" (*FI*, 19), for Kant claims that reflective judgment "cannot undertake to *classify* the whole of nature by its empirical differentiation unless it assumes that nature itself specifies its transcendental laws by some principle" (*FI*, 20). According to the transcendental principle of causality of the *Critique of Pure Reason*, each event in nature can be explained by some empirical causal law. But there could be so many empirical causal laws due to the diverse contents of experience that our finite intellect would never comprehend them all. The reflective principle of specification makes it a rule for our judgment that the various empirical causal laws should show a certain affinity when their content is coordinated. We can discover this affinity through a process of classifying empirical causal sequences, but this itself presupposes that the category of causality can be specified.

The reflective specification of the universal concept of causality is not in terms of temporally ordered objects of sense subsumed under it, but in terms of other concepts contained within it. Reflective judgment is concerned with the specification of universal concepts of the understanding *as* concepts, in order to make it possible to classify objects into a system of genera and species. The concern to systematize experience had already been dealt with in the *Critique of Pure Reason* through the regulative use of the ideas of reason. But a regulative use of reason is merely "hypothetical" (*C1*, A647/B675). Kant's efforts in the *Critique of Judgment* to reconceive the problem of systematization through "a transcendental principle" (*C3*, intro., iv, 16) of reflective judgment are aimed at overcoming the hypothetical character of systematization.

The reflection operative in the systematization of knowledge is more than comparison in the service of inductive generalization, for Kant indicates that the highest genera sought for classification are attained through the specification of our most universal concepts, i.e., the categories. Thus, the consideration that different genera of beings exist in nature requires the specification of the concept of causality into various possible kinds. After first reminding us of the central claim in the *Critique of Pure Reason*—that according to the understanding "every change has its cause" and can in principle be given an objective location in "the succession [in time] of the determinations of one and the same thing"—Kant goes on to say that "objects of empirical cognition are determined in many ways other than by that formal time condition" (*C3*, intro., v, 19).

Here we have a first indication that the successive temporal form of inner sense is not adequate for reflective judgment in general, for in the case of the cognitive use of reflection, categories such as causality are not merely to be schematized in terms of the abstract linear form of time of the first *Critique*. Since the concept of nature in general is to be articulated into "specifically different natures" (*C3*, intro., v, 19), e.g., organic and inorganic, what is required is a conception of time that permits us to imagine these different natures as coexisting. Such a conception will be developed in the next chapter, on the sublime, where the imagination comprehends what exists simultaneously (see also chapters 5 and 6).

The specification of universal concepts in the *Critique of Judgment* raises the possibility of reflecting on nature as a system of harmoniously coexisting parts. The idea of specifying a general concept suggests that Kant now regards it as a content to be formed instead of as a form that is fixed. Thus instead of considering the category of causality as a formal universal *under* which all objects of nature must be subsumed, the imagination now specifies it into "different kinds of causality" (*C3*, intro., v, 21) appropriate to different kinds of objects. Whereas determinant application was called a mechanical process in which the universal remains fixed, reflective specification was called artistic because the universal concept is itself modified: the content thought to be contained *in* the universal is specified in terms of genera and species.

Aesthetic Form and Cognitive Purposiveness

The idea of reflective specification has pointed to the fact that the form-content distinction functions in at least two ways in Kant's philosophy. From the epistemological standpoint of the first *Critique* the content of knowledge is provided by the senses and the form by the mind. A priori claims about knowledge are therefore primarily formal in nature. This involves a reversal of the traditional assumption that matter precedes form as the determinable awaits its determination. Kant is willing to admit that for things-in-themselves matter precedes form, but for the phenomenal objects perceived by us "the form of intuition (as a subjective property of sensibility) is prior to all matter (sensations)" (*C1*, A267/B323).

In the *Critique of Judgment* Kant's approach to form is no longer tied to the problem of the possibility of experience but to that of "the possibility of experience as a system" (*FI*, 18). He now considers content, not the raw material provided by the senses, but what has already been synthesized by the cognitive faculties, including the imagination. Rather than impose an a priori form on the matter of sense, reflective judgment coordinates the "natural forms" (*FI*, 17n) that can be discerned through comparing the contents of experience. The relation of matter to form is reconceived as that of the generic to the specific when Kant remarks that the Aristotelian school "called the *genus* matter, but the *specific difference* the form" (*FI*, 19n). In reflective specification we regard nature as a genus that must be specified into different species of objects. In this limited sense, matter again precedes form, but only for the heuristic purpose of coordinating different species into one coherent system.

In Hegelian language, this kind of form that differentiates one species of objects from others would have to be characterized as a concrete or individuating form. But specification as a function of reflective judgment cannot make any constitutive claims about nature and its objective forms. The only constitutive use of reflective judgment is aesthetical and subjective. This raises the question, how is *aesthetic* form to be conceived? Is the aesthetic form of objects as apprehended by the imagination concrete?

Unfortunately, Kant's descriptions of aesthetic form are indistinct and varying. For example, he writes, "Every form of the objects of sense (both of external sense and also mediately of inner sense) is either figure (*Gestalt*) or play (*Spiel*). In the latter case it is either play of figures (in space, viz. mimetic art and dancing) or the mere play of sensations (in time)" (*C3*, §14, 61; V, 225). To define aesthetic form by the term figure suggests that it is distinct and fixed in quality, but the reference to play has the opposite effect. The aesthetic impression of a play of figures or sensations can be, at best, indeterminate. Kant also speaks of delineation as essential to the beautiful arts, only to add that ornamentation, if this too is formal in nature, can "augment the satisfaction of taste" (*C3*, §14, 61). Delineation in the mimetic art of landscape painting would demand that the objects represented be definite in outline. Ornamentation would allow these outlines to be interrupted.

What Kant says about aesthetic form in such discussions does not really move it beyond simple perceptual form. Accordingly, aesthetic form is often treated in terms derived from the problems of ordinary experience. Kant himself invites such an approach when he describes the relation between the aesthetic form of objects and the cognitive faculties as one of "harmony which is requisite for empirical cognition" (*C3*, intro., vii, 28). Thus, for example, Ralf Meerbote regards aesthetic forms as the "invariant features of apprehended manifolds"[20] that not only produce aesthetic pleasure but are also necessary for the production of knowledge.[21]

By concentrating on only those elements of aesthetic apprehension that can be construed as necessary for the conformity between aesthetic and ordinary cognitive judgments, we can easily be led to the conclusion that much in Kant's aesthetic theory is implausible or inadequate. As Meerbote points out, if his interpretation of aesthetic form as the invariant features of apprehended manifolds is correct, then "Kant may have to declare *all* sense-perceptible objects beautiful."[22]

Instead of seeking a stipulative definition, a more fruitful approach to Kant's conception of aesthetic form is to focus on how it functions in the reflective framework of aesthetic judgment. Aesthetic form is not intuited empirically by means of the synthesis of apprehension, but is apprehended by the imagination conceived as the "faculty of a priori intuitions" (*C3*, intro., vii, 26). In the aesthetic judgment, imagination does not perform its normal perceptual task, but assumes an a priori judgmental function. Thus what is apprehended in aesthetic

20. Ralf Meerbote, "Reflections on Beauty," in *Essays in Kant's Aesthetics,* eds. Ted Cohen and Paul Guyer (Chicago: University of Chicago Press, 1982), 79.
21. Theodore Uehling defines aesthetic form as the "spatial and temporal relations exhibited by a synthesized manifold." See *The Notion of Form in Kant's Critique of Aesthetic Judgment* (The Hague: Mouton, 1971), 58. Mary McCloskey speaks of "forms final for perception" that "cannot complete the activity of perceiving, [but] must invite and sustain it." See *Kant's Aesthetic* (London: Macmillan Press, 1987), 71.
22. Meerbote, "Reflections on Beauty," 81.

form is not just a perceptual shape, but a purposiveness. This purposiveness apprehended in the form of an object is the a priori element contributed by the imagination in its play with the understanding. Here the imagination functions in accordance with a "transcendental principle which represents a purposiveness of nature . . . in the form of a thing" (*C3*, intro., viii, 31). This purposiveness can be attributed to the form of an object either aesthetically without a concept or teleologically with a concept. Concerning nonconceptual aesthetic purposiveness, Kant writes: "Purposiveness may be represented in an object given in experience on a merely subjective ground as the harmony of its form—in the apprehension (*apprehensio*) of it prior to any concept—with the cognitive faculties, in order to unite the intuition with concepts for a cognition generally (*überhaupt*)" (*C3*, intro., viii, 29; V, 192). Kant considers this purposiveness of aesthetic form for "a cognition generally" to be a subjective purposiveness, for no determinate knowledge is being produced. This purposiveness without a purpose is contrasted with the objective purposiveness of the teleological judgment. Whereas in the case of the aesthetic judgment the form of the object precedes any concept of what the object ought to be, in the case of the teleological judgment a concept of what a thing ought to be "precedes and contains the ground" of its form (*C3*, intro., viii, 29). The teleological judgment makes a cognitive claim, although it is only reflective and regulative. Its use of form is conceptually specified to differentiate one kind of organic system from others.

The aesthetic judgment can be a constitutive mode of reflective judgment, but it dispenses with any definite cognitive claim. A purely aesthetically apprehended form is not a differentiating form which would serve to specify an object cognitively. It can, however, be suggestive for the more general process of reflective specification. The aesthetic judgment is constitutive for feeling (see *C3*, intro., ix, 34) in producing a pleasurable harmony of the faculties that is purposive for cognition generally.

From Kant's descriptions of aesthetic form and harmony we can distinguish two ways in which the cooperation of the faculties can be cognitively purposive.[23] In relation to what is required for all determinate empirical knowledge, the play of the imagination and the

---

23. We shall see in chapter 5, however, that aesthetic harmony is not to be conceived purely in terms of cognitive purposiveness.

understanding is one of "accord" or "attunement" (*Stimmung*). In the judgment of aesthetic form the cognitive faculties are brought "into that proportionate accord or attunement which we require for all cognition" (*C3*, §9, 54; V, 219). It is the accord necessary for all cognition that is appealed to in the deduction of taste to assure that aesthetic judgments can be universal.

Most discussions of Kant's conception of aesthetic form and harmony tend to focus on the relation of accord or attunement necessary for determinate knowledge, but the more significant purposiveness relates to the requirements for "cognition in general (*Erkenntnis überhaupt*)" (*C3*, §9, 52; V, 217), which includes the reflective concern with the systematization of knowledge.[24] Thus Kant also speaks of a "state of mind in the free play of the imagination and the understanding (so far as they are in agreement with each other [*zusammenstimmen*], as is requisite for *cognition in general*)" (*C3*, §9, 52; V, 218). Here the two faculties attain the mutual "agreement" necessary for reflective specification.

Whereas in a proportionate accord the imagination and the understanding may stand in a fixed but unequal ratio, in a mutual agreement they are equal partners that must adapt to each other. The *accord* necessary for *all* cognition and the *agreement* necessary for cognition *in general* can be correlated with the two ways in which Kant said the categories may be presented or specified, i.e., either mechanically through application or artistically through reflection. We found initially that there was an *accord* between apprehension and presentation that could be understood by looking back at the way categories are schematized by the imagination in the first *Critique*. This accord represents the extent to which "reflection already has its guide in the concept of nature in general, i.e., in the understanding, and the judgment requires no special principles of reflection, but *schematizes* these concepts a priori" (*FI*, 17). But reflection begins to require its own transcendental principle when it proceeds to specify this general concept of nature and sets itself the task of the systematic ordering of the empirical content of nature. Thus to understand fully the aesthetic

24. Friedrich Kaulbach also distinguishes "cognition in general" from all determinate cognition. But whereas I interpret "cognition in general" to refer to the reflective concerns of knowledge, Kaulbach defines it as a special mode of aesthetic world-knowledge that involves a self-world perspective. See *Ästhetische Welterkenntnis bei Kant* (Würzburg: Königshausen und Neumann, 1984), 27.

apprehension of form it must also be related forward to the overall systematic concern of reflective judgment. In this case the relation between apprehension and presentation is an *agreement* felt between the apprehended form of an object and the reflective specification of the categories.

It is the purposive agreement between imaginative apprehension and the presentation of the specified concept of nature that is felt, however dimly, when we find pleasure in an aesthetic form. But the pure aesthetic form of an object cannot itself be specified so as to delimit it from other objects. Only the teleological judgment makes it possible to differentiate certain classes of objects, i.e., organisms that can be regarded as individuated systems with their own internal organization. In the aesthetic judgment, the pleasing form merely gives us hope that nature as a whole can be systematized.

In the case of beautiful forms in nature, Kant says explicitly that they are like "ciphers (*Chiffreschrift*) through which nature speaks to us figuratively" (*C3*, §42, 143; V, 301). This way of describing beauty in nature brings out an affinity between mathematical form and aesthetic form. We saw in chapter 2 that when mathematical ciphers are deciphered by the monogrammatic imagination, they disclose the basic spatial patterns of the phenomenal world. Aesthetic forms are also called ciphers because in their own way they suggest the overall systematic structure of the world. When judging a humanly created beautiful form we must, according to Kant, "become conscious that it is art and not nature" (*C3*, §45, 149). But this difference does not in any way affect the kind of purposiveness that is felt, for Kant continues by writing: "Yet the purposiveness in its form must seem to be as free from all constraint of arbitrary rules as if it were a product of mere nature" (*C3*, §45, 149). Both in the case of natural and artificial beauty, the purposiveness felt refers to the overall order of our experience.

Examples of beautiful form are commonly drawn from Kant's discussion of flowers and ornamentations, where it is easy to make light of Kant's simple taste for tulips and wallpaper designs. A more instructive example can be found in §58, where Kant speaks at length of "the crystalline configurations of many minerals" that "present beautiful shapes, the like of which art could have invented (*ausdenken*)" (*C3*, §58, 194; V, 349). The formation of crystalline structures can be explained mechanically as the result of a determinate specification or sudden solidification of fluids in accordance with the laws of nature. But Kant's suggestion that a crystal is like a work of art allows us to regard it as if it were teleological, i.e., as if its purposiveness were based on some prior concept. To that extent aesthetic form becomes specifiable. The crystal can be regarded as an individuated system that is like a microcosm of the overall order of things. Whereas the form of a tulip is mainly characterized by delineation or outline, a crystalline configuration is formed throughout and thus provides a better aesthetic prototype for the reflective specification of the categories necessary for the systematization of nature. We can also speak of "crystallization" as a metaphor for a process by which the vague or fluid play of the imagination and the understanding is suddenly captured in a form.[25]

Aesthetic apprehension suspends the normal reading of the manifold of sense and does not produce the objective meaning of experience that we found in chapter 2. Of the flowers and "free delineations" that Kant considers to be beautiful, he writes that they "have no meaning (*bedeuten nichts*), depend on no definite concepts, and yet they please" (*C3*, §4, 41; V, 207). Although beautiful forms are mere ciphers and carry with them no determinate meaning, they possess a value or significance. Whereas mathematical ciphers have a value that can be determined numerically, aesthetic ciphers can at best be assigned an indeterminate felt value. To decipher the significance of a beautiful form is to read between the lines of the ordinary experiential reading of nature and to find in some objects a "trace (*Spur*)" or a "hint (*Wink*)" (*C3*, §42, 143; V, 300) that nature may be in general agreement with the needs of reflective judgment.

The indeterminate significance or subjective purposiveness of an aesthetic form is felt as a harmony of the cognitive faculties that can be communicated, not through concepts, but through a common or communal sense (*Gemeinsinn*). This common sense that communicates through feeling is the ultimate postulate of aesthetic judgment. It not only goes behind the intellectual conditions for knowledge established in the first *Critique,* but also points beyond the general reading of nature that this *Critique* made possible. The reading of nature that gives objects a mathematical meaning only assures us that

25. Cf. Ernst Cassirer, *Kant's Life and Thought,* trans. James Haden (New Haven: Yale University Press, 1981), 315.

every relation among the properties of objects is governed by some law. But, as we indicated earlier, there could be so many discrete laws that the meanings assigned to objects could still be so varied that no coherent or systematic interpretation of nature would be possible. Then the overall meaning of experience would remain abstract despite the fact that the schemata of the imagination assign meaning to particular objects. The search for a unified meaning (*Bedeutung*) would be defeated by the multiplicity of what is spelled out in sense (*Sinn*). In the aesthetic judgment the object—the flower, for example—loses its meaning only to point back to a more fundamental common sense (*Gemeinsinn*). This common sense places the flower, which has been removed from its immediate experiential relations, into a subjective communal context more fundamental than an objective context.

The full import of Kant's theory of common sense—the value of common sense in orienting us to the totality of what can be known through science, both natural and social—will be examined in chapter 8. All that need be said here is that while the transcendental conditions of natural science which were explicated in the first *Critique* can be demonstrated to be necessary for everyone's experience, the transcendental reflective conditions explicated in the third *Critique* can be imputed to everyone only insofar as they are concerned with the overall order of things. The concern to systematize nature is just one manifestation of this, but one that at the same time makes clear the role of communication, for no complete system of science is possible without a community of scientists.

If aesthetic pleasure were based on the syntheses of apprehension and reproduction or on the invariant features of apprehended manifolds, it would be a most predictable aspect of experience, based on associations. But Kant denies the applicability of *empirical association* of sense to judgments of taste. Instead, such pure aesthetic judgments disclose what might be called a *transcendental sociability* of common sense. Everyone could, but not everyone will, develop these transcendental conditions within himself, and that is why the capacity to apprehend aesthetically is unpredictable. It has the unexpected value of finding an imaginative analogue to the reflective process of specifying universal concepts. Apprehending a formally organized object encourages us to hope that nature as a whole can be systematically organized.

We have seen that the aesthetic imagination is not limited to the preliminary, precognitive functions often assigned it, but plays a role in reflective judgment's systematic concern with knowledge in general. In explicating the harmony of the faculties involved in the pure aesthetic judgment, we have focused on that aspect of the imagination's purposiveness that points beyond the production of empirical knowledge to its possible integration. The free conformity of the aesthetic imagination to the understanding allows it to dispense with empirical concepts, but not the categories. Indeed, its greatest contribution to reflective judgment lies in suggesting that such universal concepts can be specified to organize the content of our experience.

4
The Regress of the Imagination:
The Sublime and
the Form of the Subject

Although most accounts of the aesthetic judgment in the *Critique of Judgment* have focused on the Analytic of the Beautiful, some of the more significant developments in Kant's theory of the imagination occur in the Analytic of the Sublime. The greater freedom and scope given to the imagination in the Analytic of the Beautiful are further increased in the Analytic of the Sublime.

The concept of the sublime, so popular in the eighteenth century, has long since been viewed as peripheral to aesthetics. There has been a continued interest in the moral import of the sublime, but this has led to the neglect of its more general theoretical significance.[1] Yet Kant's reflections on the sublime provide important clues for relating aesthetic consciousness to the overall economy of our mental powers. In raising the possibility of an aesthetic mode of comprehension, Kant introduces a feature of the imagination's activity which contrasts with its previously assigned functions. So far the imagination has been linked to the understanding, either to help it synthesize the progressive sequence of representations in time or to help specify its general concepts. In relation to the sublime, by contrast, the imagination is claimed to institute a "regress" that annihilates the conditions

1. One of the few exceptions is J. F. Lyotard, who claims that from the postmodern perspective, modern art found its "impetus" in "the aesthetic of the sublime." (Jean-François Lyotard, "Answering the Question: What Is Postmodernism?" in *The Postmodern Condition: A Report on Knowledge,* trans. G. Bennington and B. Massumi [Minneapolis: University of Minnesota Press, 1984], 77.) The difference between the modern and the postmodern is characterized by their respective responses to the sublime or the unpresentable. Modern aesthetics "allows the unpresentable to be put forward only as the missing contents"; the postmodern aesthetic, by contrast, "puts forward the unpresentable in presentation itself" (Lyotard, "Answering the Question," 81). What was unpresentable because it transcended the accepted forms of discourse becomes presentable or imaginable when artists are willing to violate these forms. It should be added that when the imagination violates forms its products are not readily communicable and require interpretation.

of time and is related not to concepts of the understanding, but to ideas of reason. This imaginative regress is important for comprehending as a whole what is normally apprehended as temporally discrete.

Aesthetic comprehension and the regress of the imagination are central features in the Analytic of the Sublime, and point to a possible integration of the faculties that Kant had left separate in the first two *Critiques*. Some of Kant's efforts in this direction lead him into metaphysical speculation. However, I shall contend that the results of the imaginative regress in the sublime can be interpreted in essentially transcendental terms.

The Sublime and Aesthetic Comprehension

The sublime is introduced in the *Critique of Judgment* as a state of mind elicited by the representation of boundlessness or the infinite. Its characteristic feature, according to Kant, is a "movement of the mind" whose subjective purposiveness is referred by the imagination either to the faculty of cognition or to the faculty of desire (*C3*, §24, 85). The Analytic of the Sublime is therefore divided into two sections: (1) the *mathematical* sublime, which is related to the cognitive faculties and represented in terms of magnitude, and (2) the *dynamical* sublime, which is related to the faculty of desire and represented in terms of might or power. The moral and religious themes most commonly associated with the sublime are emphasized in the latter section.

The less familiar account of the mathematical sublime contains theoretical discussions of the general structure of our consciousness of the sublime, and it is here that we see new points of departure for a theory of the imagination. Although the imagination is usually conceived as a mode of sensuous apprehension, it is now claimed to have also the power of aesthetic comprehension. Moreover, the imagination is clearly revealed to be a function of judgment as well as a faculty of sense and thus to be capable of establishing a measure for itself.

Kant opens his discussion of the mathematical sublime with some comments about magnitude in general and points to a significant aesthetic element in the judgment of magnitude. He argues that the objective mathematical measurement of magnitude by means of number ultimately presupposes an aesthetic estimate of magnitude. Numbers are defined mathematically in terms of a unit which cannot in turn be defined numerically. The concept of number not only has a pure intuitive content produced by the imagination as the faculty of a priori intuition, but also presupposes a given intuitive measure or form as its standard. This form is not empty like time and space; in contrast to the normal Kantian view, it appears to be both sensuous *and* absolute. Whereas numbers present "relative magnitude by means of comparison," the intuitive measure "presents magnitude absolutely" prior to any comparison (see *C3*, §26, 90).

> The estimation of the magnitude of this fundamental measure must consist in this, that we can immediately prehend or grasp (*fassen*) it in intuition and use it by the imagination for the presentation of concepts of number. That is, all estimation of the magnitude of the objects of nature is ultimately aesthetical (i.e. subjectively and not objectively determined). (*C3*, §26, 89; V, 251)

In addition to the immediate prehension (*Fassung*) of the fundamental measure in intuition, Kant distinguishes two activities of the imagination necessary for mathematical measurement: apprehension (*Auffassung*) and comprehension (*Zusammenfassung*). The imagination can use the fundamental measure as a unit to generate a numerical sequence where each added unit is apprehended successively. Or, as it proceeds numerically, the imagination can also construct more encompassing units of measure, as in a scale where ten or even a hundred units may be comprehended as one. This second operation of the imagination, which is designated as *"comprehensio aesthetica"* (*C3*, §26, 90), allows us to move from a simple fundamental measure to a more encompassing measure. However, this is not an unlimited process, for as apprehension advances "it loses as much on the one side as it gains on the other" (*C3*, §26, 90).

Imaginative apprehension is identified with the mathematical estimation of magnitude and imaginative comprehension with its aesthetical estimation. On the basis of what Kant asserts about this mode of apprehension, I will call it "mathematical apprehension" and make the preliminary observation that it is more akin to the synthesis of apprehension of the first *Critique* than to the apprehension of aesthetic form discussed in the previous chapter. Like the synthesis of apprehension in intuition, mathematical apprehension is empirical and uses concepts. It has nothing to do with the a priori but nonconceptual apprehension of purposiveness in aesthetic form.

According to Kant, mathematical apprehension "can go on *ad infinitum*," but for aesthetic comprehension "there is a maximum beyond which it cannot go" (*C3*, §26, 90). When the imagination's capacity to intuit simultaneously a series of units reaches a limit, aesthetic comprehension encounters the immeasurable and the feeling of the sublime. This maximum, "if it is judged as the absolute measure than which no greater is possible subjectively . . . brings with it the idea of the sublime and produces that emotion which no mathematical estimation of its magnitude by means of numbers can bring about (except so far as that aesthetical fundamental measure remains vividly in the imagination)" (*C3*, §26, 89–90).

The sublime as the absolutely great is "great beyond all comparison" and can be projected only insofar as we remain conscious of the absolute fundamental measure that underlies numerical measurement. This is a condition that is commonly overlooked in discussions that focus only on the immeasurable in the sublime. The judgment of the sublime involves a polar relation between (1) the limit of aesthetic prehension, which is an absolute lying at the basis of all comparison, and (2) the limit of aesthetic comprehension, which is the absolutely great beyond all comparison. Thus, the imagination contains a simultaneous reference to an absolute measure and the immeasurable. This bipolar reference is a characteristic which we will come upon in other forms as we explore further the operations of the imagination.

So far, in this preliminary discussion of the sublime, we have seen that the imagination has been assigned the dual function of apprehension and comprehension. Apprehension can be described as a process that advances or progresses, so that to apprehend a magnitude is to grasp it part by part in a temporal succession. The comprehension of a magnitude involves the more difficult task of grasping or judging it as a whole. Thus Kant asks whether comprehension is possible when we are looking at something massive, such as a pyramid: "If we are very near, the eye requires some time to complete the apprehension of the tiers from the bottom up to the apex, and then the first tiers are always partly forgotten before the imagination has taken in the last, and so the comprehension of them is never complete" (*C3*, §26, 90).

The problem of comprehension illustrated by observing a pyramid recalls that encountered in the *Critique of Pure Reason,* for given his assumption of the temporal spread of the processes that constitute experience, the grasping of a complex whole poses a particular difficulty for Kant. In both the first and third *Critiques,* he appeals to the imagination to deal with the discreteness of what is apprehended in inner sense, but the solutions as well as the contributions of the imagination differ in significant respects. The differences are due in large measure to the fact that in the third *Critique* the theory of the imagination includes the idea of an aesthetic comprehension.

The pyramid example is reminiscent of the line example used in the Subjective Deduction to show the need for a synthesis of reproduction. As we saw, Kant argued that if I cannot reproduce the first parts of a line as I advance to those that follow, I cannot obtain a complete representation. But reproduction itself would be in vain if I could not recognize that all the different parts of the line belong to one total unit. This recognition of unity requires a conceptual synthesis through a concept of number. (See our more detailed analysis in chapter 1.)

In the Analytic of the Sublime Kant refers back to this numerical unity obtained by the synthesis of recognition as "*comprehensio logica* in a concept of number" (*C3,* §26, 93). This logical, but really mathematical, comprehension is to be distinguished from the *comprehensio aesthetica* in which the imagination unites several representations in one intuition without the mediation of mathematical concepts.

It should be repeated here that any act of aesthetic comprehension must still conform to the synthetic conditions established by the unity of apperception and the categories. In the case of the aesthetic apprehension of the form of an object we only denied the applicability of empirical concepts. It would follow, therefore, that the mathematical categories are still applicable to aesthetic comprehension and that only the specific numerical concepts necessary for a synthesis of recognition can rightfully be excluded. In this respect aesthetic comprehension resembles the aesthetic apprehension of form. Neither act requires the special syntheses of the imagination discussed in the first *Critique.*

The main difference between aesthetic apprehension and aesthetic comprehension seems to lie in their respective scope. Kant refers aesthetic apprehension to the form of relatively simple objects, such as flowers and decorative patterns. Aesthetic comprehension, by contrast, is related to more complex, composite objects, such as the pyramids or the altar in St. Peter's. The problem of perceiving a set of coexisting objects was first raised in Kant's precritical discussion of the synoptic city-image (see chapter 1). It was then exacerbated in the first *Critique,* where the temporality of consciousness is thought to mean that the apprehension of one thing excludes the simultaneous apprehension of another. For if the form of inner sense is linear and represents everything in succession, how do we become aware of several things at the same time? According to Kant, "The synthesis of imagination in apprehension would only reveal that the one perception is in the subject when the other is not there, and *vice versa,* but not that the objects are coexistent" (*C1,* B257). In the *Critique of Pure Reason* it was clearly Kant's view that the imagination by itself cannot grasp the coexistence of objects in space. The fact that we do experience the coexistence of things was accounted for by the assumption that they stand in a relation of reciprocal interaction. That is, the knowledge of coexisting objects in nature presupposes the concept of causal reciprocity, which is the third of Kant's relational categories.

Given our assumption that not only the mathematical categories but also the dynamical categories are employed in reflective judgments, it would seem that the difference between logical and aesthetic comprehension lies in how each specifies the category of reciprocal causality. In the case of logical comprehension this category is applied in terms of empirical concepts that synthesize what has been apprehended piecemeal by the imagination. By contrast, aesthetic comprehension seems to specify the category of reciprocity by reshaping time itself. This suggests that the imagination can directly intuit coexistence by stopping the forward flow of time. Such a shift in conceiving time may be correlated with a shift from the needs of the understanding to those of reason.

The understanding, to which the imagination has been related so far, functions discursively; it needs a progressive, linear form of time to run through the contents of sense one by one. In the Analytic of the Sublime, Kant expands the role of the imagination by considering it in relation to reason, which functions holistically. Whereas the understanding is the faculty of finite knowledge, reason strives to comprehend the infinite. The mere ability to think the sublime "shows a faculty of mind surpassing every standard of sense" (*C3,* §25, 89). The imagination, of course, cannot encompass the infinite, yet in relation to the mathematical sublime it is induced to strive for a kind of completeness that calls for a reconsideration of its relation to time.

The Regress of the Imagination

The nature of aesthetic comprehension is most fully revealed when the imagination reaches its maximum, i.e., when it encounters the "absolutely great" as an idea of reason. The imagination, in an unexpected reversal of its normal operation, institutes a "regress" which suspends the progressive sequence of apprehension in inner sense and makes possible the intuition of coexistence. This is described in a key passage:

> The measurement of space (regarded as apprehension) is at the same time a description of it, and thus an objective movement in the act of imagination and a progress. On the other hand, the comprehension of multiplicity (*Vielheit*) as a unity—not of thought but of intuition—and consequently the comprehension in an instant (*Augenblick*) of what was successively apprehended is a regress which annihilates (*aufhebt*) the condition of time in this progress of the imagination and makes *coexistence* intuitable. It is therefore (since the time series is a condition of inner sense and intuition) a subjective movement of the imagination, by which it does violence to inner sense. (*C3*, §27, 97–98; V, 258–59)

This regress annihilating the "condition of time" represents a departure from the position we saw clearly established in Kant's first *Critique;* and the question is, does the "violence to inner sense" contradict that position?

A link between the imagination and a progressive form of time was shown to be necessary for making objective and determinant judgments about nature. However, for aesthetic judgment as a mode of reflective judgment the mathematical determination of nature is not at issue; it does not require the numerical progression of time that is based on the spatial analogy of a measurable line. But the fact that temporal determinacy is not necessary for aesthetic consciousness in the way that it is for cognitive consciousness still does not account for the more radical claim that the imagination violates inner sense and annihilates the condition of time. If Kant is here positing a mode of intuition that transcends time, then this would mean a violation of the critical framework. However, I would argue that the regress of the imagination does not annihilate time as such, but merely suggests the possibility of negating the mathematical or linear form of time. This can be explicated through an examination of some of the significant terms in the passage quoted above.

The imaginative regress which annihilates the condition of time is said to be a "comprehension in an instant (*Augenblick*)" of what was successively apprehended. In both the Bernard and Meredith translations of the *Critique of Judgment* this is rendered as comprehension "in one glance."[2] But *Augenblick* has a technical meaning which is better brought out by translating it as "instant" or "moment."[3] In the first *Critique*, Kant identifies an instant (*Augenblick*) as a limit of the time continuum. An instant limits time in the same way a point limits space (see *C1*, A169/B211). Just as space consists of spaces, not of points, so time consists of times, not of instants. Therefore, an instant is not a self-subsisting constituent of time, but is a limiting point of the time line. In this light, the annihilation of the condition of time in the regress of the imagination may be interpreted to limit time rather than transcend it, so that the regress involves, in Schiller's words, "annulling time within time."[4] Thus instead of the linearly ordered time required for the progressive apprehension and mathematical determination of nature, we have an instant or moment in time which allows for aesthetic comprehension and reflection.

On this interpretation of the annihilation of time, it is in one sense more difficult to account for Kant's other claim that the regress of the imagination "makes coexistence intuitable." We know from the first *Critique* that an instant is not sufficient to allow us to apprehend the manifold contained in a given intuition, for the apprehension requires temporal discrimination. Every intuition, Kant writes, "contains in itself a manifold (*Mannigfaltigkeit*) which would not be represented as a manifold if the mind did not distinguish time in the sequence of one impression upon another" (*C1*, A99; IV, 77). In fact, "each representation, *insofar as it is contained in a single instant (Augenblick), can never be anything but absolute unity*" (*C1*, A99; IV, 77). Given these claims, how can the regress be a "comprehension in an instant" and also provide an intuition of coexistence?

2. *C3*, §27, 98; see also *Critique of Judgment*, trans. J. C. Meredith (Oxford: Clarendon Press, 1964), part 1, 107.

3. Since writing this chapter, I have received the new translation by Werner Pluhar, who also uses the term "instant." See *Critique of Judgment*, trans. Werner S. Pluhar (Indianapolis: Hackett Publishing Co., 1987), 116. Unfortunately this translation came too late for me to use it more extensively in this manuscript.

4. Friedrich Schiller, *On the Aesthetic Education of Man*, trans. E. M. Wilkinson and L. A. Willoughby (Oxford: Clarendon Press, 1967), 97. With fuller exploration, Kant's suggestion also invites comparison and contrast with Husserl's *epoché* on the one hand and Heidegger's *Augenblick* on the other.

In the passage on the imaginative regress, Kant does not elaborate on the nature of the coexistence that is instantaneously comprehended, but his terminology indicates that the conceptualization of the plurality-unity relation in aesthetic comprehension differs from that in logical comprehension. We have, in Kant's words, "the comprehension of multiplicity (*Vielheit*) as a unity." Here he uses the term *Vielheit* (multiplicity) instead of the more familiar word *Mannigfaltigkeit* (manifold). In logical or mathematical comprehension the content of sense is regarded as a manifold, i.e., a complex of temporally determined parts. In aesthetic comprehension, by contrast, the content of sense is regarded as a multiplicity of *indeterminate* parts of a whole. The unity of the former must be inferred by means of a concept and involves the objective progress of the imagination. The unity of the latter can be instantaneously comprehended in the subjective regress of the imagination.

The differences between *Vielheit* and *Mannigfaltigkeit* are lost in the Bernard translation of the third *Critique*, where both terms have been rendered as "manifold" (§27, 97),[5] thus giving the misleading impression that the imaginative regress is dealing with the "comprehension of the manifold" reserved for the conceptual syntheses of the understanding. In fact, the imaginative regress is dealing with the comprehension of a multiplicity as a unity. The shift from "manifold" to "multiplicity" is significant for the analysis of the imagination vis-à-vis the nondeterminant reflective judgment.

The differentiation between multiplicity and manifold is also implicit in the Anticipations of Perception of the first *Critique*, where Kant distinguishes between extensive and intensive magnitudes. An extensive magnitude involves a manifold generated by a successive synthesis proceeding from parts to whole. By contrast, an intensive magnitude is not apprehended successively, but in an instant. Intensive magnitude, which is identified as a degree, represents the multiplicity in the content of sense. Kant writes:

> A magnitude which is apprehended only as unity, and in which multiplicity (*Vielheit*) can be represented only through approximation to negation = o, I entitle an *intensive* magnitude (*CI*, A168/B210; III, 153).

Paton interprets this obscure passage to mean that the multiplicity in an intensive magnitude is not represented by parts outside one an-

---

5. The same is true for the Meredith translation (107). Again, this is corrected in the new Pluhar translation (116).

other. Instead, "every degree contains a plurality, because it contains all lesser degrees down to zero."[6] The multiplicity involved is not of discrete parts of a manifold, but of degrees of intensity.

This multiplicity in unity is given in an instant; yet, apparently, it can be represented *as* a multiplicity only when we imagine a possible diminution of the sensation. Such an imaginative act would require a process in time, and is not easily squared with Kant's assertion that the apprehension of intensive magnitude through sensation is instantaneous. This difficulty is part of a more general one posed by the Anticipations of Perception. As Robert Paul Wolff has pointed out, the entire argument of the Anticipations appears out of harmony with Kant's main line of argument concerning transcendental synthesis.[7] Certainly in the context of the first *Critique,* an instantaneous *synthesis* through which we intuit multiplicity remains at best problematic.

With the further development of the theory of the imagination in the third *Critique,* the intuition of multiplicity is more readily conceivable through a *nonsynthetic regress* of the imagination which annuls the linear form of time. We saw that the estimation of aesthetic magnitude is a condition for the determination of mathematical magnitude, and involved both apprehension and comprehension by the imagination. Whereas apprehension relates unit to unit in the time sequence, aesthetic comprehension intuits multiple units of measure as coexistents in an encompassing measure of magnitude. The unity that is thus aesthetically comprehended in an instant is neither the "absolute unity" of an instantaneous sensation nor the "synthetic unity" obtained through empirical concepts in logical or mathematical comprehension. The "absolute unity" of a sensation anticipates something real corresponding to it, thus giving access to what exists as a *"realitas phaenomenon"* (*C1,* A168/B209). The "synthetic unity" of experience provides a conceptual unity for the manifold of sense in terms of objects that endure over time. The unity of aesthetic comprehension is both more encompassing than a sensation and less determinate than the experience of objects.

The first contrast—that between aesthetic comprehension and sensation—can be explicated by means of our earlier distinction between

6. Paton, *Kant's Metaphysics* (see chap. 2, n. 1), vol. 2, 136, n. 1.
7. Cf. Robert Paul Wolff, *Kant's Theory of Mental Activity* (Cambridge: Harvard University Press, 1963), 235.

aesthetic prehension and aesthetic comprehension. Aesthetic prehension is the act of grasping the "absolute unity" of a sensation, and therefore must have an intensity that measures instantaneously "a degree of influence on sense" (*C1*, A166/B208). Aesthetic comprehension by contrast measures what I would call an instantaneous confluence of sense. Whereas aesthetic prehension has as its correlate intensive magnitude as a measure of *existence*, aesthetic comprehension provides the measure for *coexistence*.

The second contrast—that between aesthetic comprehension and ordinary experience—can be explicated by our distinction between a multiplicity and a manifold. Experience requires the successive ordering of what is given to sense as a linear manifold in order to represent (*vorstellen*) objects determinately. Aesthetic comprehension is content to present (*darstellen*) multiplicity as an indeterminate unity. Simultaneous aesthetic presentation involves a loss of determinacy.

Kant illustrates these features of aesthetic comprehension when he explains what makes the sight of the starry heavens and the ocean sublime. We must regard them merely as we see them. If we approach them cognitively, and think of them as populated with living creatures, then no feeling of sublimity will be aroused. We must regard them "merely by what strikes the eye (*Augenschein*)" (*C3*, §29, III; V, 270)—the starry heavens must be seen as an "all-embracing vault," the ocean as either "a clear mirror" if it is calm or as "an abyss threatening to overwhelm everything" if it is restless (*C3*, §29, 110, 111).

Paul de Man finds in these descriptions of the sublime a "disarticulation" of nature into "the pure materiality of *Augenschein*"[8] and an absence of unity rather than the indeterminate unity that I have claimed. While the linear reading of nature is suspended by the regress of the imagination, it does not, as de Man thinks, disintegrate into the "prosaic materiality of the letter"[9] in which the living meaning of ordinary experience collapses into the dead letter of routine language. The *Augenschein* that is comprehended in an *Augenblick* has no materiality at all. The sublime view of the ocean offers a pure surface that abstracts from the living contents of the ocean, but relates back to the unity of our own life (see chapter 5).

8. Paul de Man, "Phenomenality and Materiality in Kant," in *Hermeneutics: Questions and Prospects,* eds. Gary Shapiro and Alan Sica (Amherst: University of Massachusetts Press, 1984), 143.
9. de Man, "Phenomenality," 144.

The Whole Determination of the Mind

The conception of aesthetic comprehension which has been developed through our interpretation of the regress of the imagination reflects the generally more holistic approach that is discernible in the third *Critique*. Although Kant usually treats the faculties of mind separately, his analysis of the sublime leads us to consider the subject as a whole and the ground for conceiving its coexisting faculties as a unity. Kant points in this direction in the concluding sentence of the passage on the regress. The annihilation of time in the imaginative regress is contrary to purpose for inner sense, but, he asserts, "that very violence which is done to the subject through the imagination is judged as purposive *in reference to the whole determination* of the mind" (*C3*, §27, 98).

Kant's dealings with the relation of the faculties in the sublime suggest a greater reciprocity among the faculties. We noted earlier with reference to the Analytic of the Beautiful that the imagination's subordinate role to the understanding was modified into a more indeterminate, spontaneous relationship. Aesthetic pleasure in beauty consists in the harmonious play of the two cognitive faculties. In the sublime, it is reason and imagination qua faculty of sense which are compared and related—not through their harmony, but through their conflict. The feeling of the sublime is dual in nature. It involves displeasure as the imagination recognizes that it is incapable of comprehending absolute greatness, and pleasure insofar as this recognition serves the purpose of disclosing the power of reason in the *same* subject. The imagination's "own incapacity (*eigne Unvermögen*) uncovers the consciousness of an unlimited capacity or faculty of the same subject" (*C3*, §28, 98; V, 259).

The displeasure and the pleasure exist simultaneously (*zugleich*) in the feeling of the sublime. However, at one point the duality of feeling is characterized as an *Erschütterung*, a convulsive movement or violent feeling that shakes us (See *C3*, §27; V, 258). Because Kant says that this movement may be compared to a quickly alternating repulsion and attraction of a convulsion, it may appear that he is in effect defining the displeasure and the pleasure in the sublime as successive rather than simultaneous. But the comparison with a convulsion is used only as an image for the movement, "especially in its beginnings" (*C3*, §27, 97). Kant's full analysis indicates that he maintains the simultaneity of the displeasure and pleasure in the feeling of the sublime (*C3*, §27, 98), and our preceding discussion of the imaginative regress has shown that in its instantaneous comprehension the imagination is no longer held to the successive form of time. The overall effect of the sublime is that of a "negative pleasure" (*C3*, §23, 83).

The two conflicting feelings would cancel each other if one of them were not felt to be purposively related to the other. Representations that are judged to be purposively related are not juxtaposed in a mere mechanical succession, but are felt to coexist. One is comprehended by virtue of the other. In the sublime, the conflict between sense and reason makes for a consciousness of their coexistence in the same subject. This conflict is purposive in that it "arouses in us the feeling of our supersensible destination (*übersinnlichen Bestimmung*)" (*C3*, §27, 97; V, 258).

The idea of the supersensible destination is most frequently identified with the moral purposiveness of the sublime. However, since we are focusing primarily on the theoretical implications of the mathematical sublime, our present concern is with the idea of the supersensible as it relates to the problem of the overall determination of the mind.[10] As Kant tells us in the Dialectic of Aesthetic Judgment, he had sought in the supersensible "the point of union for all our *a priori* faculties" (*C3*, §57, 187).

In considering the supersensible as a ground of unity, Kant may appear to be moving beyond the purely epistemological analysis of the relation among the faculties and into the realm of transcendent metaphysics. For example, his appeal to the supersensible has been seen as an effort to provide a metaphysical ground of taste.[11] Admittedly, there are some passages in the third *Critique* that might justify such interpretations, for Kant is, after all, dealing with an idea which has been prevalent in traditional metaphysics. However, within the framework developed in the sublime, the idea of the supersensible

10. It should be noted, in this regard, that the word *Bestimmung* as in the phrase *übersinnlichen Bestimmung* can also mean "determination." The latter meaning was used in the first quotation in this section, where it was claimed that the imaginative regress is purposive for "the whole determination of the mind (*die ganze Bestimmung des Gemüths*)" (V, 259).

11. Paul Guyer gives one of the best arguments for this point of view in *Claims of Taste* (see chap. 3, n. 8), 340. See also Robert L. Zimmerman, "Kant: The Aesthetic Judgment," in *Kant: A Collection of Critical Essays*, ed. Robert Paul Wolff (Garden City, N.Y.: Doubleday & Co., 1967), 385–406.

may be treated transcendentally; it functions as a transcendental condition disclosed by the regress of the imagination. When so conceived, the idea of the supersensible may be used in a transcendental philosophy of mind to ground a theory of the subject as a whole. This would be in keeping with Kant's evident interest in raising aesthetic judgments of the sublime "out of empirical psychology" and bringing them "into transcendental philosophy" (*C3*, §29, 106).

The regress of the imagination annihilates the linear time produced by the transcendental imagination of the first *Critique*. Yet this regress can be seen to have a transcendental character itself when compared with Kant's account of the cosmological regress. In his translation of the third *Critique*, Bernard refers the regress of the imagination to the System of Cosmological Ideas of the first *Critique* where Kant speaks of a "regressive synthesis" of reason. However, there are some important differences between the two kinds of regress.

The cosmological regress is one of reason's speculative efforts to transcend experience in its search for an absolute objective totality. That is, reason harbors the illusion that if the conditioned in nature is given, then the entire series of conditions of nature must also be given. As Kant puts it, "What reason is really seeking in this serial, regressively continued, synthesis of conditions, is solely the unconditioned" (*C1*, A416/B443–44). Here reason misconceives time by thinking that it can go back to a beginning of time and accumulate all the conditions of our experience of nature serially. The regressive synthesis of reason extends the imagination beyond its limits to create the illusion of totality.

By contrast, the regress of the imagination in the sublime does not involve a temporal synthesis; it is instantaneous. Moreover, instead of extending the imagination beyond its limits, it provides the occasion for the imagination to reflect on them. In the presence of the sublime, the imagination qua faculty of sense compares itself with reason and "exhibits its own limits and inadequacy" (*C3*, §27, 96). When confronting the absolute greatness of the sublime, the imagination institutes a regress to reason which is not so much transcendent as transcendental.

Conceived as transcendental, the regress could explain why Kant claims that the exposition of judgments of the sublime "was at the same time their deduction" (*C3*, §30, 124). The exposition of the movement of the imagination from apprehension to comprehension can be seen to have a structure analogous to the movement in the Subjective Deduction from the synthesis of apprehension to the syntheses of reproduction and recognition. Each of these syntheses reaches a limit which requires an appeal to the succeeding synthesis and ultimately back to a transcendental principle of unity. What starts as a progressive movement ends up as a regress. By pushing to expand its role from apprehension to comprehension, the imagination recognizes its empirical limits from within and observes its relation to the transcendental unity of reason itself. If this recognition of limits is made evident in the very exposition of the sublime, then it in fact needs no separate deduction.

Unlike the cosmological regress, the regress of the imagination in the sublime is not directed to the objective determination of the absolute, but is a subjective movement to what Kant calls a "supersensible substrate":

> That magnitude of a natural object on which the imagination fruitlessly spends its whole faculty of comprehension must carry our concept of nature to a *supersensible substrate* (*übersinnliches Substrat*) (which lies at its basis and also at the basis of our faculty of thought). As this, however, is great beyond all standards of sense, it makes us judge as *sublime*, not so much the object, as our own state of mind in the estimation of it. (*C3*, §26, 94; V, 255; first emphasis added)

The idea of a supersensible substrate of nature points both above sense and below nature, and appears to be, in Wolff's phrase, "the last word in mixed metaphors."[12] For Kant, the supersensible usually designates the intelligible, or what transcends experience. As described in the context of the regress of the imagination, however, the idea of the supersensible substrate contains a reference to the transcendent that serves to disclose the transcendental conditions of the judging subject. In conjunction with the rational idea of our destination we are carried back to the supersensible substrate, which Kant described as the common "basis" for both our concept of nature and our faculty of thought. Kant distinguishes three ideas of the supersensible in the Dialectic of Aesthetic Judgment:

1) the supersensible in general, "as the substrate of nature";
2) the supersensible "as the principle of the subjective purposiveness of nature for our cognitive faculty"; and

---

12. R. P. Wolff, *Mental Activity*, 224, n. 2.

3) the supersensible "as the principle of the purposes of freedom."
(C3, §57, 191)

Of these three ideas, two are metaphysical and not relevant to the regress of the imagination. The first denotes the noumenal reality
which defies the theoretical knowledge sought by speculative metaphysics. This idea of the supersensible substrate can be identified with
the absolute conditions of reality aimed at but never attained in the
cosmological regress of the *Critique of Pure Reason*. There is no reason
to think that the regress of the imagination is more successful in
providing access to the noumenal reality of nature. The only
noumenal reality about which we have the right to make claims is that
of our own moral nature. This relates to the third idea of the supersensible and the purposes of freedom. While the *Critique of Practical
Reason* does show that a metaphysics of morals may legitimately postulate freedom as necessary for morality, it also makes clear that the
imagination has no positive role in such a metaphysics. The imagination is not assigned any function in schematizing the moral law. It is
unlikely therefore that the regress of the imagination in the mathematical sublime gives access to the noumenal in the moral sense.

The remaining or second idea of the supersensible "as the principle
of the subjective purposiveness of nature for our cognitive faculty" is
the principle of reflective judgment and the one relevant to the regress
of the imagination. This principle, which is central to the *Critique of
Judgment,* has already been appealed to in chapter 3 and can be reformulated in terms of our present concerns. The principle of reflective
judgment requires us to assume "that nature specifies its universal
laws according to the principles of purposiveness for our cognitive
faculty, i.e., in accordance with the necessary business of the human
understanding of finding the universal for the particular which perception offers it" (C3, intro., v, 22). It is necessary to assume that we
can find in nature not only the specific empirical laws for every phenomenon, but also the higher unifying principles that connect the
various empirical laws into a comprehensive rational system. This involves a "transcendental principle," Kant asserts, which "reflective
judgment can only give as a law from and to itself" (C3, intro., iv, 16).
The principle is not metaphysical because it does not attempt to determine what nature is in itself, but only posits a purposive, subjectively
necessary link between nature and ourselves.

Thus the supersensible substrate disclosed in the regress of the sublime is a transcendental idea that allows us to assume the mutual purposiveness of nature and the subject in aesthetic judgments. This purposiveness was already recognized as a feature of judgments of beauty. But the sublime is equally important for developing the full reciprocity of the relationship between nature and the subject. Kant writes in the introduction that there is "not only a purposiveness of the objects in relation to the reflective judgment by virtue of the concept of nature in the subject, but also conversely a *purposiveness of the subject* in respect of objects according to their form or even their formlessness by virtue of the concept of freedom. Hence the aesthetical judgment is not only related . . . to the beautiful, but is also . . . related to the *sublime*" (*C3*, intro., vii, 28–29; V, 192, first emphasis added).

In sum, the beautiful and the sublime are both necessary aspects of aesthetic judgments because together they reveal the mutual purposiveness of nature and consciousness implicit in the supersensible as the transcendental principle of reflective judgment. Whereas our judgments of beauty are made with reference to a purposiveness of the object, judgments of the sublime involve a "purposiveness of the subject." Reflection on beauty leads us to hope for a greater harmony and systematic order in nature; the sublime points to the possibility of an overall integration of our faculties of mind.

The Form of the Subject

The purposiveness of the subject, as dealt with in the mathematical sublime, focused on the cognitive faculties. In the dynamical sublime, subjective purposiveness is referred to the faculty of desire, and the supersensible destination is directly discussed in moral terms. Here the imagination functions in the service of practical reason, that is, in relation to the third idea of the supersensible—the principle of the purposes of freedom.

The moral destination disclosed in the sublime requires a comprehensive unity of the subject that relates the theoretical and practical activities of man. In the "supersensible ground," Kant asserts, "the theoretical faculty is bound together in unity with the practical in a way which, though common, is yet unknown" (*C3*, §59, 199). This unity is not demonstrated by Kant, and the satisfactory treatment of the subject as a whole remains an unfulfilled task in his philosophy. However, analysis of the structure of consciousness in the sublime may be carried further to suggest the idea of a unitary aesthetic form of the subject, and we may look to the dynamical sublime for some reflections on the human subject and the imagination which will supplement those derived from our interpretation of the mathematical sublime.

In the dynamical sublime, absoluteness is estimated, not in terms of magnitude, but in terms of might or power (*Macht*). The sheer power of nature exhibited in a hurricane or a waterfall tends to make man regard himself as insignificant. Yet it can also cause him to reflect on his own power and locate "in himself a sublimity of disposition" which is superior to mere physical power and conformable to rational law (see *C3*, §28, 103). It is important to note that an individual can only recognize the sublime and his rational, supersensible destination if he is morally cultivated. Thus Kant claims that "without development of moral ideas, that which we, prepared by culture, call sublime presents itself to the uneducated man merely as terrible" (*C3*, §29, 105).

The judgment of the sublime requires a subject to have developed himself as an individual. Like most of his eighteenth-century contemporaries, Kant considered the appreciation of beauty as akin to a social pleasure; the aesthetic judgment, as we saw in chapter 3, can be grounded in a "transcendental sociability." But the sublime designates a state of mind which, while in society, is not dependent on it. "To be sufficient for oneself, and consequently to have no need of society without at the same time being unsociable, i.e. without flying from it, is something bordering on the sublime" (*C3*, §29, 116). The regress of the imagination involved in the sublime produces, as it were, a subliminal sense of one's own resources and individuating power. Certain affections, such as enthusiasm, are deemed sublime because they arouse and strain *all* our coexisting faculties or forces (*Kräfte*), thereby disclosing the whole power (*Macht*) of our mind. The disclosure of the subject's whole power in the dynamical sublime speaks to Ernst Cassirer's point that the general significance of the idea of purposiveness in the *Critique of Judgment* lies in the possibility of defining individuating structures.[13]

13. Cf. Cassirer, *Kant's Life* (see chap. 3, n. 25), 287.

Just as the purposiveness of beauty is related to the form that de-
limits an object, so the purposiveness of the sublime implies what we
may call the form of the subject. A reference to form might be
thought inappropriate in the context of the sublime, for it is widely
interpreted to be formless. However, Kant does not write that the
sublime can be found *only* in a formless object, but that it can *also* be
found there.[14] In an earlier quote Kant indicated that the sublime involves a purposiveness of the subject "in respect of objects according
to their form or even their formlessness" (*C3*, intro., vii, 28). Thus
what is judged to be sublime is not necessarily formless. This can be
shown not only for the objects involved, but also for the state of mind.
St. Peter's Basilica, which according to Kant arouses the feeling of the
sublime, is not without form; it only seems so when we first enter because of our inability to comprehend as much form as we expect to be
there. Concerning the state of mind involved in the sublime, it is clear
that the annihilation of the mathematical form of time in the regress
of the imagination is not the annihilation of form as such. Indeed, the
violation of the form of inner sense discloses the overall form of the
subject that encompasses all its faculties. Earlier we saw that in the
mathematical sublime the imagination contains a simultaneous reference to a fundamental aesthetic measure or form and the immeasurable or absolutely great. Here in the dynamical sublime, we may say
that the imagination comprehends both the aesthetic form of the
subject and its infinite moral destination.

The imagination does not, however, produce any positive image of
either the integration of our faculties or our moral ideas. In fulfilling
its task of making itself adequate to the idea of reason, the imagination does not rely on its sensuous capacity to produce and reproduce
empirical images. The imagination in the service of reason can only
provide what Kant calls an "abstract . . . mode of presentation" of
the infinite—one that is "quite negative in respect of what is sensible"
(*C3*, §29, 115). Any effort to produce a positive representation of the
moral law or the tendency to morality in us would result in the sort of
illusions involved in the cosmological regress and the other antin-
omies of theoretical reason. In its relation to practical reason, the
imagination provides a negative presentation of morality, for "the *in-*

14. "das Erhabene ist dagegen auch an einem formlosen Gegenstande zu finden" (*C3*,
§23; V, 244). The *auch* (also) is ignored in the Bernard translation—cf. 82.

scrutableness of the idea of freedom quite cuts it off from any positive presentation" (*C3*, §29, 116). A negative presentation can elevate and expand the soul, and at the same time guard against fanaticism, which is the *"belief in our capacity of seeing something beyond all bounds of sensibility* . . . (or of going mad with reason)" (*C3*, §29, 116).

We have seen how the negativity of the imagination in annihilating the condition of time allows us to remain in time without remaining subject to its sensuous determination. We now see that the negativity of the imagination's abstract presentations opens us up to the determination of reason without subjecting us to its illusions. Although the imagination cannot develop a positive image of our moral destination, it does induce reflection on our rational, moral powers. In this context, the third idea of the supersensible, as the principle of the transcendent purposes of freedom, is used reflectively to develop the immanent purposiveness of the human subject.

However much the imagination is used to serve reason in the sublime, aesthetically it remains a function of reflective judgment. As such, it must draw back from the kinds of limitless goals that reason can project by itself. In the sublime, therefore, the imagination presents our supersensible destination, not only as morally transcending nature, but also as the human form of nature in us. The judgment of the sublime has "its roots in human nature" (*C3*, §29, 105), and the imagination may project only within the limits of human possibility.

Ultimately, the "determining ground" of all aesthetic judgment is located in what Kant calls the "supersensible substrate of humanity" (*C3*, §57, 185). This substrate of humanity also underlies the *sensus communis* (common sense) which is the transcendental principle of the judgment of beauty. Thus the concept of humanity provides the basis for aesthetic judgments through which form is elicited from the content of experience, rather than imposed upon it. And as we have seen, the sublime makes a significant contribution to this by disclosing the overall human form of the subject.

We have suggested the possibility of a transcendental philosophy of mind in which the imagination can play an essential role. Thus in addition to the formative, synthetic, and reflective activities already ascribed to it, the imagination can establish a regress that uncovers certain transcendental conditions of mind. In so doing, the imaginative regress has been shown to overcome the problem of temporal discreteness and to produce an aesthetic, as distinct from a logical, comprehension. This instantaneous aesthetic comprehension allows us to intuit coexistence as a unity of indeterminate parts. It is through such aesthetic comprehension that we may best grasp the unity of the finite and the infinite that characterizes the human subject in the feeling of the sublime.

This unity of the finite and the infinite is anticipated in the conclusion of the *Critique of Practical Reason,* where Kant writes, "Two things fill the mind with ever new and increasing admiration and awe, the oftener and more steadily we reflect on them: the starry heavens above me and the moral law within me."[15] The infinitude of the starry heavens annihilates my importance and underscores my finitude. Yet by locating the moral law within me I enhance my own value. The starry heavens can be sublime only insofar as I recognize my infinite moral destination. This recognition is, according to Yovel, Kant's Copernican revolution "in microcosm."[16] We tend to be more impressed with the infinity of physical nature than with the infinite destiny of our moral nature, and the consciousness of the sublime is necessary to reverse this distorted evaluation. The Copernican revolution of the first *Critique* proved that concepts of the *understanding* rather than things-in-themselves set the conditions of objectivity; that of the second *Critique* showed that the authority of the moral law derives not from without, but from within each person's *reason.* The third *Critique's* revolutionary transposition of view occurs in the regress of the *imagination* in the sublime: the inability of the imagination to comprehend mathematical infinity produces a regress that allows us to feel a sublime infinity within ourselves. This regress is best understood transcendentally as the basis for an integration of the faculties. If it is also to be interpreted metaphysically as the basis for a metaphysical link between the phenomenal and the noumenal, it is a link that is given only in feeling. But as we shall see in the next chapter, one of the greatest metaphysical mysteries—the fact that matter can at times partake of life—must be approached through feeling.

15. Kant, *Critique of Practical Reason* (hereafter *C2*), trans. Lewis White Beck (Indianapolis: Bobbs-Merrill Co., 1956), 166.

16. Yirmiahu Yovel, *Kant and the Philosophy of History* (Princeton: Princeton University Press, 1980), 131.

5
The Life of the Imagination

The development of the imagination's powers that we have seen in the judgments of beauty and the sublime can be more fully comprehended when related to the idea of life that informs the third *Critique*. Although it has been overlooked by most commentators, the idea of life provides an overall perspective for understanding the reflective functions of the imagination.

When Kant defines the subjective nature of aesthetic judgments, he adds the significant, but largely unnoticed specification that representations are referred to the subject's feeling of life (*Lebensgefühl*). This feeling, like aesthetic feeling in general, is not reducible to a private state with a particular psychological content; it is formal in nature and in principle universally communicable. Nor is the term "life" limited to its biological meaning; it is used more broadly to convey a sense of vitality that also encompasses our mental life. The idea of life can thus be used to point to the fundamental coherence of the two parts of the *Critique of Judgment*. Goethe has written in admiration of the *Critique of Judgment*: "Here I saw my most disparate concerns brought together, artistic and natural production treated in the same way and the powers of aesthetic and teleological judgment mutually illuminating each other."[1] However, Kant does not explicitly state on what basis aesthetic and biological phenomena can be linked.

According to Ernst Cassirer, the fundamental connecting theme of the two halves of the *Critique of Judgment* is that of creation, which manifests itself both in art and in organic life. He writes, "Aesthetic intuition discerns that interpenetration of formative forces on which the possibility of the beautiful and the possibility of life equally rest;

---

1. Johann Wolfgang Goethe, "Einwirkung der neuern Philosophie," in *Goethes Werke* (Weimar: Hermann Böhlau, 1893), part 2, vol. 11, 50.

for the phenomenon of beauty and that of life both are comprised and enfolded in the single underlying phenomenon of creation."[2] This interpretation, which makes the creative imagination central to the *Critique of Judgment,* is faced with a difficulty, for most of the Critique of Aesthetic Judgment deals with the problem of taste rather than creativity. The aesthetic imagination has so far been characterized as spontaneous and playful, but not as creative. Its primary functions are related to the disinterested apprehension of the forms of objects, in the case of beauty, and to the comprehension of the coexistence of things, in the case of the sublime. The discussion of artistic creation occurs relatively late in the Critique of Aesthetic Judgment, when Kant turns to the consideration of genius. The theme of creation may serve as an interpretive bridge between the two halves of the *Critique* insofar as Kant concludes the first part with a discussion of artistic productivity and moves on to organic productivity in the Critique of Teleological Judgment. It does not, however, constitute a pervasive theme underlying the *Critique* as a whole.

Kant's idea of life is commonly associated with his discussion of teleological judgments concerning biological phenomena.[3] But contrary to expectation, the term "life" and its cognates occur more frequently in the Critique of Aesthetic Judgment than in the Critique of Teleological Judgment.[4] Indeed it is possible to interpret the overall structure of the *Critique of Judgment* as one whereby the idea or sense of life is gradually explicated. Aesthetic judgment is rooted in a subjective feeling of mental life; teleological judgment articulates individual objective forms of organic life. It is this idea of life that may well account for Goethe's appreciation and that makes Kant an unrecognized precursor of the Goethe-Dilthey tradition of using the imagination to understand the meaning of life. Life, as Dilthey declared, is an ultimate, behind which we cannot go. While Kant is less explicit than Dilthey in articulating a concept of life, the third *Critique* shows

2. Cassirer, *Kant's Life* (see chap. 3, n. 25), 279.

3. See Reinhard Löw, *Philosophie des Lebendigen* (Frankfurt a. M.: Suhrkamp, 1980), chaps. 3, 4.

4. One of the few to have commented on Kant's reflections on life within an aesthetic context is Barbara Zeldin in "Pleasure, Life and Mother-Wit," in her *Freedom and the Critical Undertaking: Essays in Kant's Later Critique* (Ann Arbor: University Microfilms International, 1980), 116–139. Friedrich Kaulbach interprets the feeling of life as a self-world consciousness that provides a special kind of aesthetic world-knowledge. See his *Aesthetische Welterkenntnis* (see chap. 3, n. 24), 7.

him repeatedly referring to a feeling of life to elucidate some of his basic concepts.[5]

Aesthetic Pleasure and the Feeling of Life

Before turning to the idea of life in the *Critique of Judgment,* we should briefly mention three earlier works where Kant gives an explicit definition of life. In the early essay "Dreams of a Spirit-Seer" (1766) Kant writes, "I am very much inclined to assert the existence of immaterial natures in the world, and to put my soul itself in that class of beings."[6] Anything living, he adds, "seems to be of immaterial nature. For all life rests on the inner capacity to determine one's self by one's free choice (*Willkür*)" (*DSS,* 52–53n; II, 327n). While any human knowledge of spirits must be denied, claims about the life of souls— however speculative—can be correlated with what Kant calls the observable "free movement" (*DSS,* 57) of bodies in this world. Another definition of life appears in the *Metaphysical Foundations of Natural Science* (1786) where Kant seeks to clarify the concept of inertia as life-lessness. In contrast with inertia, life is "the capacity of a substance to determine itself to act from an internal principle, of a finite substance to determine itself to change, of a material substance to determine itself to motion or rest as change of its state" (*MFNS,* 105). It is clear that Kant is here speaking speculatively, for the last part of this metaphysical definition is immediately called into question. Since matter is claimed to be lifeless, it is doubtful whether any material substance can be said to have the capacity to determine itself. In the *Critique of Practical Reason* there is a footnote in which Kant gives a brief psychological interpretation of the above definition. Life is now given a more limited meaning as "the capacity of a being to act according to the laws of the faculty of desire" (*C2,* 9n).

As these comments indicate, Kant had spoken of life prior to the *Critique of Judgment,* but it is the first work in which he repeatedly uses the idea of life as part of his main text. Yet he does not give a specific definition of life, except to say that both life and the principle

---

5. Dilthey himself seems to have been unaware of Kant's aesthetic appeals to the feeling of life.

6. Kant, *Dreams of a Spirit-Seer, Illustrated by Dreams of Metaphysics* (hereafter *DSS*), trans. Emanuel F. Goerwitz (New York: Macmillan, 1900), 52.

of life can be identified with mind (*Gemüth*) (see *C3*, §29, 119; V, 27). "Mind" seems to be used here as a descriptively neutral term that makes no claims about either souls or spirits.[7] By equating mind and life, Kant suggests a broader understanding of life than appears in his preceding definitions, which focused on life as a self-determining or self-motivating activity. We will see that life must involve not only the capacity to act, but also the consciousness of being acted upon. The latter engenders a capacity to respond, which is crucial to the *feeling* of life in the *Critique of Judgment*.

In the opening section of the *Critique of Judgment* Kant defines aesthetic pleasure in terms of the feeling of life. A representation is aesthetic if it "is altogether referred to the subject *and to its feeling of life*, under the name of the feeling of pleasure or pain" (*C3*, §1, 38; emphasis added). From this we see that throughout his discussion of aesthetic judgments, the feeling of pleasure or displeasure is tied to the feeling of life. Pleasure is defined by Kant as the feeling of the furtherance of our life and displeasure as the feeling of the restriction of our life.[8] This holds not only for material sensuous pleasures, but also for pure aesthetic pleasure. Thus Kant writes that the beautiful "directly brings with it a feeling of the furtherance of our life, and thus is compatible with charms and with the play of the imagination" (*C3*, §23, 83). The reference to charms may seem to indicate that Kant is here merely introducing an empirical sense of biological life. But all that Kant says is that the pleasantness of charm is compatible with the pure pleasure of beauty. That is, the formal aspects of a beautiful object may be accompanied by other life-enhancing pleasures derived from the sensuous charms of the content of the object. Pleasure is always for Kant the feeling of the enhancement of the life of the subject as a whole, whether the source of the pleasure be the pleasant, the beautiful, or the good.

Kant's claim that aesthetic pleasure is disinterested means that I must be indifferent to the existence of the object judged. My indifference to the existence of the aesthetic object means that it does not satisfy any of my empirical interests. The aesthetic object could as well be a purely imaginary object, for "I am concerned, not with that

7. In Kant's *Anthropology* the question of the soul is suspended. Although Kant continues to use the idea of spirit in the *Critique of Judgment*, it is no longer in the reified sense of a kind of being, but as a principle of life.

8. See also Kant, *Vorlesungen über Metaphysik* (see chap. 1, n. 8), XXVIII, 586.

in which I depend on the existence of the object, but with that which I make out of the representation in myself" (*C3*, §2, 39). What I make out of an aesthetic representation in myself must also not depend on any prior empirical interests; nor may it produce any new interests, no matter how pure, for this would transform an aesthetic state of mind into an action that can be judged in moral terms. What I make out of an aesthetic representation gives it a purposiveness without having a specific purpose.

An important, though generally unrecognized, feature of this purposiveness without a purpose is its life-enhancing character. Aesthetic pleasure heightens the sense of my existence, furthers my feeling of being alive, and is therefore significant. While the disinterestedness of aesthetic pleasure involves an indifference to the existence of the object judged, it does not require me, the judging subject, to be indifferent to my own existence. For how could I be expected to be indifferent to the furthering of the sense of my own existence which is inherent in aesthetic pleasure?

The play of the imagination in the judgment of beauty serves to intensify the activity of our mental life in general. But because the aesthetic imagination is most often considered in relation to the cognitive concerns of the understanding, the more general life-enhancing character of its activity is easily overlooked. To the extent that the play of the imagination and the understanding establishes a "proportionate accord" required for all cognition, Kant can point to a possible justification of the universality of taste (see chapter 3). However, aesthetic consciousness itself involves not only this "accord" and an "agreement" necessary for the systematization of cognition in general, but also a "harmony" by which "the mental powers are enlivened."[9] It is this enlivening harmony which constitutes the pleasure in the overall vitality of our mental life and which encompasses more than the relation between the imagination and the understanding. Aesthetic harmony is the feeling of life at its purest, i.e., as pure mental spontaneity.

The subjective purposiveness of aesthetic pleasure is characterized in section 12 as an inner causality which serves to "preserve without further design or purpose the state (*Zustand*) of a representation"

---

9. See *C3*, §9, 54; V, 219: "die . . . durch wechselseitige Zusammenstimmung *belebten* Gemüthskräfte" (emphasis added).

(*C3*, §12, 58; V, 222). "We *linger* over the contemplation of the beautiful because this contemplation strengthens and reproduces *itself*"
(*C3*, §12, 58; last emphasis added). Here Kant uses the language of
preservation and self-reproduction that is often used by biologists to
describe organic life. However, the difference is that Kant is speaking
of mental life only. As we will see later, the life of the mind becomes
the basis for attributing organic life to nature.

The passages about preserving the state of a representation and aesthetic contemplation reproducing itself stand in marked contrast to
the analysis of time and consciousness in the *Critique of Pure Reason*.
There representations were conceived as discrete, momentary items
in the successive flow of time. Here, however, Kant focuses, not on
the representation as an intuitive content, but on the "state (*Zustand*)
of a representation," i.e., the state of mind called up by the representation. This aesthetic state of mind can last by reproducing itself
without any acts of imaginative synthesis. Thus we can distinguish
the synthesis of reproduction of the first *Critique* from the aesthetic
self-reproduction of the third *Critique*. In the former, the imagination recalls a representational content that has disappeared in the
succeeding moment; in the latter a formal response to a representation persists over a period of time. As in the regress of the
imagination in the sublime we find that the normal flow or "flowing
away (*Verfliessens*)" (*C1*, A170/B212; III, 154) of time in the first *Critique* is altered. In the case of the instantaneous comprehension
involved in the sublime, the time flow is suspended, as it were; in the
case of the lingering inherent in the contemplation of beauty, the passage of time is slowed.

In chapter 3 we indicated that the successive temporal form of inner
sense is adequate for determinant judgments of experience, but not
for reflective judgments in aesthetics. In chapter 4 we saw that the linearly ordered time of inner sense is canceled in the sublime. This was
interpreted to mean that the cognitive linear model of inner sense
must be supplemented with a nonlinear model of inner sense in the
Critique of Judgment. Although Kant continues to use the term "inner
sense (*innere Sinn*)" throughout the third *Critique*, his claim for an
instantaneous aesthetic comprehension of coexistence requires a revised conception of inner sense. A different, nonlinear model of time
and inner sense, one that can encompass what is simultaneous as well
as what is successive, is called for.

Although Kant does not directly acknowledge this need, he suggests a slightly different but related solution to the problem in his *Anthropology from a Pragmatic Point of View* by distinguishing between "inner sense (*sensus internus*)" and an "interior sense (*sensus interior*)."[10] This distinction, which is also relevant to our theme of the feeling of life, is formulated as follows: "We distinguish between inner sense, which is a mere power of perception (of empirical intuition), and the feeling of pleasure and displeasure—that is the responsiveness (*Empfänglichkeit*) of the subject in being determined by certain representations, either to preserve or to reject the state of the representations—which could be called the *interior sense* (*inwendigen Sinn*)" (*AP,* §15, 32; VII, 153).

The term "inner sense" is normally understood to mean the way consciousness apprehends what is given to it. But in the *Anthropology* Kant defines it more specifically as "the consciousness of what we *undergo* insofar as we are affected by the play of our own thought" (*AP,* §24, 39). This parallels the second edition of the *Critique of Pure Reason,* where inner sense is defined as the subjective but concrete nexus of everything we undergo as determined by the understanding.

The new conception of interior sense (*inwendigen Sinn*) is to be distinguished from both the passivity of inner sense and the activity of the understanding. The interior sense designates an intermediate, responsive mode of consciousness which involves a sensitivity of feeling to the state of the subject. Thus Kant continues by asserting that certain representations can be both sensed and felt; they are sensations that at the same time arouse "an attentiveness to the state of the subject" (*AP,* §15, 32; VII, 153). With the awareness of the state of the subject through interior sense, there is a responsiveness in terms of either affirming or rejecting the state of the representation.

It is clear that the feeling of enhanced vitality of the subject involved in aesthetic pleasure belongs to this interior sense. The relation to the feeling of life also suggests a connection between interior sense and what Kant calls the "vital sense." Like the outer senses, the vital sense is physiological, but it is not dependent on a specific bodily organ. Each of the outer senses is localized in the nerves of a

---

10. Kant, *Anthropology from a Pragmatic Point of View* (hereafter *AP*), trans. Mary J. Gregor (The Hague: Martinus Nijhoff, 1974), §15, 32.

specific organ such as the eye, but the vital sense involves those more generally encompassing sensations that pervade the entire system of the body. "The sensations of heat and cold, even those that are aroused by the mind (e.g. by quickly rising hope or fear), belong to *vital sense*. The feeling of terror that comes over us by the representation of the sublime, and the gooseflesh with which fairy tales send children to bed late at night, are vital sensations; they permeate the body so far as there is life in it" (*AP,* §16, 33; VII, 154). Whereas inner sense synthesizes the discrete givens of the five outer senses, the interior sense may be said to respond to the content of vital sense. This relation between the interior sense and the vital sense is not explicitly made by Kant, but it is apparent that both refer to our overall state of being. The interior sense attends to the overall state of the mind, the vital sense to the overall state of the body. The fact that in a *Reflexion* from the years 1775–77 Kant calls what is here conceived as the vital sense an "interior animal sense (of feeling one's body) which concerns heat and cold, languor (relaxation) and exertion" (*RA,* 290; XV, 109) lends support to our interpretation linking feeling, interior sense, and vital sense.

Adding this dimension to Kant's discussion of consciousness makes it possible to distinguish between judgments that refer to the vitality of the subject and those that refer to the existence of objects in nature. While determinant judgments affirm or negate the existence of objects in nature, reflective judgments in aesthetics may be said to affirm or negate the vitality of the subject.

Having related the aesthetic feeling of pleasure to an interior sense which attends to the mental life of the subject as a whole and responds accordingly, we can now clarify why Kant describes the contemplation of beauty as "*restful*" (*C3,* §24, 85). The idea of restful contemplation may appear to conflict with our characterization of aesthetic pleasure as vital and enlivening, but in several *Reflexionen zur Anthropologie* Kant makes it clear that a restful state of mind is not incompatible with specific powers being active. Indeed, he asserts that the mind *must* be at rest if it is to purposefully move all other powers (see *RA,* 1490; XV, 740; 1775–78, and *RA,* 1515; XV, 854; 1780–89). The life of the mind as a whole can be described as restful even though particular faculties are active. Rest in this sense does not entail passivity, but a state of equilibrium in which particular activities are balanced. On this interpretation the feeling of pleasure in beauty would provide an interior sense of an overall equilibrium in the mental life of the subject, an equilibrium which has a restorative function.

In contrast to the restful state of beauty, the characteristic feature of the sublime is said to be a "*movement* of the mind" (*C3,* §24, 85). The dual nature of the sublime cannot be understood in terms of the interior sense alone, but requires us to refer to the vital sense as well. Although the sublime does not produce as pure a feeling of mental life as does beauty, it may be said to *deepen* our sense of life. Kant writes that the feeling of the sublime "is a pleasure that arises only indirectly; viz., it is produced by the feeling of a momentary restriction of the vital powers (*Lebenskräfte*) followed instantly by an even stronger outflow of them; it seems to be an emotional state of being stirred (*Rührung*) which the imagination takes seriously, rather than as play" (*C3,* §23, 83; V, 245). The restriction of the vital powers does not of course produce a feeling of pleasure. In the case of the mathematical sublime there is no pleasure when the imagination has to admit a limit to its power to comprehend a great extensive magnitude. In the dynamical sublime, natural objects or scenes are sensed to be physically overpowering and threaten to overwhelm the vital sense of our body. The sublime would have the effect of striking us with terror, as in the example from the *Anthropology,* were it not for the recognition that we possess a kind of power other than physical power, namely, the power of reason. There is, then, initially something life-threatening about the sublime, which is why Kant says that the imagination must take it seriously. Yet to the extent that the sublime forces us into ourselves and discloses a more fundamental kind of power—the moral-rational power to improve our life rather than merely to preserve it—it also produces a kind of pleasure. The sublime is not a pure pleasurable feeling, but a mixed feeling of displeasure and pleasure.

The pleasure of the sublime is claimed to be negative, yet it does have the effect of intensifying the feeling of the life of the subject. The displeasure of our vital sense gives way to a pleasure of the interior sense. The characterization of the sublime as an emotional state of being stirred (*Rührung*) helps to explain why Kant links it to the concept of movement. He claims that the sublime involves "a subjective movement of the imagination, . . . which . . . does violence to inner sense" and collapses its temporal progression into an instantaneous or momentary glance (*Augenblick*) (*C3*, §27, 98; V, 258–59). This "violence" done to inner sense in the sublime could be said to transform it into an interior sense. The inner sense through which we apprehend the objects of experience serially as part of a time line gives way to an interior sense through which we instantaneously feel the vitality of the "*whole determination* of the mind" (*C3*, §28, 98).

In tracing further the theme of life in the *Critique of Judgment* we find the next important phase in the sections on genius and aesthetic ideas in the Analytic of the Sublime.[11] Genius involves not only the general harmony between the imagination and the understanding that is required for cognition, but also a special relation among the mental faculties, which allows some individuals to think the unknowable and express the ineffable. This special relation among the mental faculties that sets some individuals apart requires what Kant calls "spirit." Kant defines spirit aesthetically as the "enlivening principle of the mind" which "puts the mental powers purposively into swing" (*C3*, §49, 157; V, 313). Similar but more detailed characterizations of spirit occur in the *Reflexionen zur Anthropologie*. There it becomes clear that spirit is not a special talent, but that which activates all talents (see *RA*, 933; XV, 414; 1776–78). "Spirit is what is truly creative, what enlivens because it is the unity (swing) from which all movement of the mind is derived" (*RA*, 1509; XV, 826; 1780–84). This conception of spirit is applied not only to the artist's mind, but also to his work when Kant writes: "The spirit of an art is a whole, a systematic method, which contains a comprehensive (*zusammenhängende*) idea" (*RA*, 1510; XV, 828; 1780–84).

Spirit for Kant is a *heightened* mode of mental life which has a unifying power. It is not merely lively or playful, but enlivening in a creative way. What should be emphasized here is that spirit has an enlivening power that unifies in terms of a comprehensive idea. The term Kant uses is *zusammenhängend*, not *synthetisch*. What is *zusammenhängend* is inherently unified; it requires no special acts of synthesis to combine or connect its manifold. What is felt through the interior sense already coheres or hangs together. Thus, when the creative imagination functions in terms of the enlivening and coherent principle of spirit, it will not need to synthesize or unify previously separate representations into a whole.

---

11. The creation of aesthetic ideas by artistic genius will be explored in chapter 6.

In section 54 of the *Critique of Judgment* we find Kant expanding his concept of life to include the "feeling of health" or of "bodily well-being" (*C3*, §54, 177, 175). He distinguishes between the satisfaction to be gained from aesthetic judgment and the gratification derived from what pleases in sensation by claiming that the latter includes not merely the enjoyment of mental life but a sense of bodily well-being as well. One could say that now the idea of life is *broadened* by being applied to the body, except that, strictly speaking, material bodies are lifeless for Kant. Thus it is that the body must be constantly enlivened or animated. This suggests that it becomes necessary to speak of the life of the mind as spirit precisely to the extent that mind is supposed to affect the body. Spirit, as will be seen in the next chapter, has its primary artistic function in expressing or *embodying* ideas.

Whereas we feel the pleasure of furthering our mental life in aesthetic play, we can only feel the furtherance of our bodily health in what Kant calls a play of sensations. Kant thus distinguishes the imaginative play involved in apprehending beauty from three other types of play which, even though they may have an intellectual content, are enjoyed because of their sensory effect on the body. These three types of play are "the *play of fortune* [games of chance], the *play of tone* [music] and the *play of thought* [wit]" (*C3*, §54, 176). All of the modes of play enliven the bodily processes. The laughter aroused by wit, for example, is claimed to move "the intestines and the diaphragm—in a word, the feeling of health (which without such inducements one does not feel)" (*C3*, §54, 177). What is of special interest in Kant's discussion of the laughter induced by wit is the way he describes it as a convulsive movement which is similar in structure to the movement felt in the sublime. Laughter involves "*the sudden transformation of a strained expectation into nothing*" (*C3*, §54, 177). The strained expectation occurs when the understanding hits upon something absurd which momentarily deceives and frustrates it, but which is then suddenly transformed into nothing. This sudden dissipation of a seemingly puzzling state of affairs does not please the understanding, but relaxes us physically and "brings about an equilibrium of the vital powers in the body" (*C3*, §54, 178; V, 333). Thus displeasure for the intellect is transformed into pleasure for the body. Being overpowered on the level of the understanding produces an outpouring of power on the level of the body, which is comparable—in structure at least—to what we found in the sublime. There the overpowering of the imagination led to the discovery of a more fundamental power, which, to be sure, was not physical but rational.

Life and Teleology

Having brought life to the level of bodily health, which Kant defines as the "equilibrium of the antagonistic vital bodily powers" (*RA,* 1539; XV, 963; 1798–1804), we are now ready to observe the transition in the *Critique of Judgment* from the aesthetical to the teleological. So far we have only spoken of life reflexively, as it is felt immediately through either an interior or vital sense—i.e., either our own mental life or the vitality of our own body. In turning to teleological judgment Kant applies our sense of life to certain objects of nature which are distinct from ourselves. Thereby the reflective idea of life takes on a cognitive dimension. To be sure, it is not cognitive in the full sense of permitting us to make determinant judgments about objects in the manner of the first *Critique*. It is not meant to explain the properties of natural objects, but merely to describe the functions of the objects. The fact that the idea of life has a descriptive rather than explanative use may make it appear to be not essentially different from the aesthetic mode of reflective judgment, which also refers to objects but is not directly cognitive. However, while aesthetic judgments describe our subjectively felt response to objects, the teleological application of the idea of life leads to what Kant calls "a description of nature" (*C3,* §79, 266).

The sense of purposiveness in teleological reflective judgments is also stronger than that purposiveness without a purpose inherent in aesthetic reflective judgments. A teleological judgment ascribes to an organism an immanent or internal purposiveness according to which *"every part is reciprocally purpose [end] and means"* (*C3,* §66, 222). Here we describe the organism by analogy with our own capacity to act according to the causality of purposes. Aesthetic judgments reflect on the way our own feeling of life is affected by outside objects; teleological judgments reflect on certain objects insofar as they can be described as functioning analogously to spirit as the self-determining principle of life.

Although the first *Critique* taught us that all objects of nature must have their ultimate *explanation* in terms of efficient causes of a mechanistic kind, Kant now adds that for certain complex organic products the only adequate *description* will be in terms of natural purposes. In such products, "every part not only exists *by means* of the other parts, but is thought as existing *for the sake of* the others and the whole" (*C3*, §65, 220). According to Kant, such an organized being is not simply a machine displaying the mechanical power to move; it "possesses in itself *formative* power (*bildende Kraft*) which it communicates to its materials though they have it not of themselves (it organizes them). Thus it possesses a self-propagating formative power" (*C3*, §65, 221; V, 374). Whereas the moving power of a machine can be explained in terms of mechanical laws, and the organization of its parts by some external artificer, the power of an organism is both formative and "self-organizing" (*C3*, §65, 220). Accordingly, Kant states that it is not enough to consider an organized product of nature as an analogon of art; we do better "if we describe it as an *analogon of life*" (*C3*, §65, 221).

However, we cannot treat organic life as a constitutive concept— we cannot attribute life to matter. When the idea of biological life is applied cognitively to objects observed by us, it can be used only regulatively. The constitutive use of life is restricted to our own self and is noncognitive. This explains why Kant ascribes vitality to our own body in terms of a noncognitive feeling. In *The Conflict of the Faculties* Kant says that one can *feel* healthy, but one can never *know* that one is healthy.[12] This does not entail that the pleasurable feeling of health is illusory. In fact, Kant says elsewhere that "pleasure and displeasure are the only absolutes because they are life itself" (*RM,* 4857; XVIII, 11; 1776–78). Not having a knowledge of one's health only means that we are not able to determine it conceptually. Pleasure as rooted in life is an absolute for feeling, just as a sensation was shown to be an absolute for aesthetic prehension in chapter 4.

Kant's description of a living organism as a formative power (*bildende Kraft*) is reminiscent of the language used in discussing the imagination's formative power in the early *Reflexionen zur Anthropologie*. There *Einbildungskraft* (the power of the imagination) was shown to be just one of many variations of a general *Bildungskraft* (formative power or faculty) (see chapter 1). But the *Critique of Judgment* suggests that the imagination does more than represent and

---

12. Kant, *Conflict of the Faculties* (hereafter *CF*), trans. Mary J. Gregor (New York: Abaris Press, 1979), 181; VII, 100.

enhance the feeling of life; the general formative power of the imagination can be interpreted to be a manifestation of life itself. Kant relates the imagination to organic life in section 67 of the *Critique of Judgment*, where he asserts that the imagination performs an indispensable life function during our sleep. There Kant makes the extraordinary claim that our imagination, which is operative in our dreams, maintains life while we sleep. In our dreaming the imagination is an "internal power of motion" without which "sleep even in a sound state of health would be a complete extinction of life" (*C3*, §67, 227). This is based on Kant's assumption that our body qua material object is lifeless and needs stimuli to keep it in motion. When we are awake, the mind receives many kinds of external stimuli which it communicates to the body. But when we are asleep, this contact with the external world is cut off, and we need an internal source of stimuli to keep the vital functions of the body going.

Kant's appeal to the imagination in dreaming is a function of the teleological use of reflective judgment. In the Critique of Aesthetic Judgment we saw him speak of the aesthetic play of the imagination and the understanding as preserving itself. This was a constitutive claim on the level of mental life. Now in the Critique of Teleological Judgment Kant speculates that the imagination performs the task of preserving life in the biological sense—a bolder claim, which can be considered, however, to be only regulative.

A further use of the idea of life occurs relative to the problem of the purposiveness of nature as a whole. Here Kant moves from the internal purposiveness ascribed to individual organisms to consider the possibility that there may also be an external purposiveness relating different species of life to each other. Recognizing the need to proceed cautiously, Kant observes that it is impossible to judge whether one thing in nature is produced for the sake of some other thing without "knowledge of the final purpose (*Endzwecks*) (*scopus*) of nature" (*C3*, §67, 225; V, 378). To know the relative purposiveness of a natural object involves knowing its place in the whole system of nature.

What is interesting here is Kant's use of the idea of life to distinguish the explanative principles underlying the metaphysical systems of nature. "To explain the purposiveness of nature," Kant writes, "men have tried either *lifeless matter* or a *lifeless God*, or again, *living matter* or a *living God*" (*C3*, §73, 239n). Kant is critical of both types of metaphysical systems, because they make determinant claims—whether negatively or positively—about life. The only proper objective application of the idea of life is reflective.

Those metaphysicians who attempt to explain purposiveness in nature on the basis of lifeless matter or a lifeless God reduce purposiveness to a product, respectively, of blind chance or fate. Kant finds these positions unacceptable, for they regard purposiveness as nothing but a subjective ideal.

Turning to the other metaphysical explanations of purposiveness, Kant warns against a "realism of the purposiveness of nature" that dogmatically asserts the hypothesis of living matter (*hylozoism*) or that of a living God (*theism*) (see *C3*, §72, 239). But he does think that a nondogmatic, or reflective, use of both ideas is necessary if we are to avoid reducing nature to a machine and God to an abstract deistic principle. That nature must be conceived so as to leave room for organic life is obviously the thrust of the Critique of Teleological Judgment. That God must be conceived as living is far from obvious in light of Kant's denial in the first *Critique* that real knowledge of God is possible for the human intellect. The attribution of life to God only makes sense in light of Kant's suggestion in section 59 of the Critique of Aesthetic Judgment that we can nevertheless have symbolic knowledge of God. Although the idea of God can never become a determinate object of experience, it can be given a kind of analogical or symbolic objectification if used reflectively.[13] We are not told what can serve as a symbol of God, but we do learn that Kant used the teleologically organized living body as a symbol for the idea of a republican state governed by laws (see *C3*, §59, 198). Because God himself is thought to personify the idea of sovereignty in relation to the rational kingdom of ends,[14] it seems reasonable to propose that a self-organizing living mind is the appropriate symbol of God. This can be indirectly confirmed on the basis of certain *Reflexionen zur Metaphysik* from the same period. According to Kant, "God is not merely a first cause, but a creator. Proof of a living God" (*RM*, 6431; XVIII, 714; 1790–95). At another point, he writes, "The psychological concept of God as *summa intelligentia* is that of a living God with understanding and will. Its proof derives from teleology, not from the

13. The function of symbolization will be explored further in chapter 6.
14. In the *Reflexionen zur Anthropologie* Kant writes: "The true sovereign of the state is the idea of a whole society and its source of power, namely, God, who realizes and personifies this idea" (*RA*, 1398; XV, 610; 1772–73).

concept of reality" (*RM*, 6439; XVIII, 717; 1790–95). Kant also re-describes the physico-theological argument so that the analogy of the artist used in the *Critique of Pure Reason* is replaced with the analogy of a "living first mover" (see *RM*, 6444; XVIII, 719; 1790–95).

By suggesting that both political and religious ideas can be represented in terms of symbols based on life, Kant may be attempting to ground them in human feeling. Since our access to life is through feeling, the idea of a state as a living body and that of God as a living mind would be ideas that we not merely project rationally, but with which we identify through our feelings. If this is the case, then the idea of a living God can be seen as setting the stage for Schleiermacher's religion of feeling.

One of the last references to life in the *Critique of Judgment* is contained in section 83, where Kant claims that human beings can be considered a genuine purpose of nature only insofar as they make something of themselves through culture. Kant considers the value of life on the basis of the distinction between natural purposes such as happiness and other purposes established by human culture. Considered in terms of our happiness, life has a mere negative value: "It sinks below zero" (*C3*, §83, 284n). But considered in terms of what we make of ourselves through the self-discipline of culture, life can have positive value: "There remains then nothing but the value which we ourselves give our life, through what we not only do, but do purposively in such independence of nature that the existence of nature itself can only be a purpose under this condition" (*C3*, §83, 284n; V, 434n). The thesis that culture can contribute to the moral dimension of life will be explored in chapter 7. For our present purpose it confirms that life is not a mere biological phenomenon to be set apart from spirit. In conceiving life, Kant does not think in terms of a dualism; organic life and the life of the mind constitute a continuum allowing a scale of positive and negative values.

Conclusion

We have seen how the idea of life pervades the entire structure of the *Critique of Judgment*, and it has been argued here that the teleological sense of life derives from its aesthetic sense—in sum, that biological life obtains its meaning from the feeling of mental life.

There is a passage in the *Reflexionen zur Anthropologie* which might appear to contradict this view. Here Kant distinguishes three modes of life: animal, human, and spiritual, and he orders them in a way which could suggest that animal life is the most basic. Animal life is said to make us capable of enjoyment or gratification (*Vergnügen*), human life of the satisfaction involved in a judgment of taste, and spiritual life of "satisfaction through reason" (*RA*, 823; XV, 367; 1776–78). Since they are compared purely on the basis of what kind of satisfaction they produce, all three modes of life involve consciousness. Animal life is thus not reducible to the organic functions of our body, but represents the way the states of our body measure the *"actus* of life" (*RA*, 823). Enjoyment is the enhancement of life as felt through the bodily organs.

In the *Critique of Judgment* Kant concedes to Epicurus that enjoyment, even if "it starts with representations of the imagination or the understanding, may ultimately be corporeal, because life without a feeling of bodily organs would be the bare consciousness of existence, without any feeling of well-being" (*C3,* §29, 119; V, 277–78). The enjoyment of animal life can now be called a feeling of well-being that is to be distinguished from life as such. Kant continues: "The mind by itself alone is life (the principle of life), and hindrance and furtherance must be sought outside it and yet in the human being, consequently in connection with its body" (*C3,* §29, 119; V, 278).

While this passage confirms my basic thesis about the mental nature of life, it also serves to create a problem by suggesting that all feelings of the furtherance of life are connected with the body and the senses. Since aesthetic pleasure was defined as the feeling of the enhancement of life, it could be argued that there is ultimately no difference between the well-being of animal life and the supposedly pure aesthetic pleasure of human life. This would be the case if the connection with the "senses" were to be conceived only in terms of specific bodily organs. But the aesthetic feeling of life was related to the interior and vital senses, which are not tied to specific sensory organs such as the eye or ear. Since the vital sense relates to overall states of the body, it is possible to feel the furtherance of life in a way that is not reducible to the gratification of the senses.

Although the senses are necessary to apprehend an aesthetic form, the ordinary sensual and perceptual interests are suspended in aesthetic contemplation. Indeed, the purity of the aesthetic feeling of life is no more compromised by the fact that it must be related to the body in a general way than is the transcendental status of "I" in the "I think" by requiring "some empirical representation to supply the material for thought" (*C1*, B423n). To be sure, in the first *Critique* Kant maintains that the "I think" is an empirical proposition because it "contains within itself the proposition 'I exist'" (*C1*, B422n). The "I" alone is purely intellectual; the *actus* "I think" involves an "indeterminate empirical intuition, i.e., perception" of my existence. Kant's subsequent comments on the transcendental ego in the *Prolegomena* suggest, however, that the "I think" and the "I exist" may be nonempirical as well. The representation of the transcendental ego (the I of apperception) is redescribed as "nothing more than the *feeling* of an existence without the least concept" (*PFM*, 82n; emphasis added). The indeterminate representation of the transcendental ego's existence is no longer conceived as an indeterminate perceptual intuition, which would make it empirical, but as a feeling, which can be pure and formal. This feeling of the existence of the transcendental ego may be none other than the pure aesthetic feeling of life, which is defined as the "bare consciousness of existence" (*C3*, §29, 119). The aesthetic feeling of life can therefore be interpreted as the subjective counterpart of the transcendental "I think." It is the transcendental feeling of spontaneity (the *actus* of life) that corresponds to the spontaneity of the intellect (the *actus* "I think"). Such an idea of transcendental feeling is anticipated in the *Prolegomena* when Kant calls life "the subjective condition of all our possible experience" (*PFM*, 83).

The idea of associating life with the transcendental conditions of human experience and action receives further support in the *Reflexionen zur Metaphysik,* where Kant defines life as movement conceived transcendentally.[15] Whether this assertion merely claims life as the fundamental condition for animate movement or also for all movement is not clear, however. In the *Opus postumum* Kant indicates that the a priori capacity of a subject to move and to initiate movement involves at the same time the capacity to "anticipate the counteracting moving forces of matter" (see *OP*, XXII, 506). This assertion makes it possible to consider life as the transcendental condition for both the power to

---

15. "Bewegung in transzendentalem *Verstande ist Leben.*" *RM,* 4786; XVII, 728; 1775–76, 1778–79.

move and to be moved, and allows us to interpret the aesthetic feeling of life as a transcendental point of unity for both the active power of the understanding and the receptivity of sense. Such an interpretation suggests a way of mitigating Kant's dualism of understanding and sense. On this view aesthetic feeling is not a mere response to the representations of either understanding or sense, but involves the responsiveness of life itself.

I have indicated that the idea of life is broadened in the *Critique of Judgment* from an abstract notion of spontaneity to a more inclusive idea of responsiveness which would make aesthetic feeling truly central to Kant's theory of mind. Whether or not this particular conclusion is accepted, the general thrust of the analysis in this chapter should make it clear that the idea of life does play a transcendental role in Kant's aesthetics. Although there are empirical ways in which life manifests itself in enjoyment through the movement of sense organs, the harmony of the faculties is itself a pure movement that directly manifests the life of the mind.

By linking the feeling of life to the interior and vital senses, we can point to a significant shift away from the essentially atomistic psychological assumptions of the first *Critique*. Inner sense, as originally conceived, had consisted of a series of discrete contents; the interior sense, the vital sense, and aesthetic consciousness are clearly holistic.

The modification of Kant's psychological assumptions that we have seen in the third *Critique* and in the *Anthropology* never calls into question his basic transcendental assumptions about the general synthetic structures of the understanding. Nevertheless, the third *Critique* has introduced a broader horizon within which to survey the operations of the imagination. In aesthetic consciousness the feeling of life gives an immediate access to the overall state of mind of the subject, so that instead of helping to synthesize representations, the imagination serves to fashion a pervasive but indeterminate unity into a more determinate unity. To a mind given discrete perceptual contents, the task is that of synthesis; but when it is given a total state or an overall continuum, the task is to make differentiations within it, that is, to articulate the structure of the continuum. The reflective specification of universal concepts that we examined in chapter 3 would be an instance of a process of articulation. Synthesis moves from parts to wholes; articulation from wholes to parts. This synthesis-articulation distinction[16] cannot be attributed to Kant himself, but it serves to indicate the direction the further development of his ideas might be taken. The rudiments of such a distinction are, in fact, clearly discernible in Kant's *Opus postumum*. There he writes that a life force "functions in accordance with ideas and moves according to an immaterial principle. It thus transcends the system of elements of the natural sciences and belongs to the concept of a world-system which must be represented as proceeding from the idea of the whole to its parts" (*OP*, XXII, 602). What Kant refers to as a "system of elements" begins with parts and, through concepts, synthetically constitutes a whole. By contrast, a "world-system" begins with an idea of the whole and is fundamentally analytical in method. A comparable distinction is made by Goethe in his description of the process of formation and transformation in organic nature: "Nature constantly observes an analytical procedure, a development from a living, mysterious whole, and then again she seems to proceed synthetically by causing seemingly alien relations to approximate each other and connecting them into a unity."[17] In Kant, the two procedures are attributed to our consciousness of nature rather than to nature itself. While the synthetical procedure was dominant in the construction of ordinary or scientific experience in the first *Critique,* the analytic procedure gains prominence in the reflective specification of concepts in the third *Critique.*

Within the holistic perspective of the *Critique of Judgment,* the aesthetic functions of the imagination discussed in this and the other chapters of part 2 have been directed to the articulation of the overall purposive relations that are inherent in our felt response to the world. In part 3 the imagination's functions will be examined for their contribution to interpretation, for as we saw in chapter 2, interpretation only becomes possible when we have a sense of the world as a whole.

16. I first used this distinction to clarify Dilthey's methodological approach to the human sciences. See Makkreel, *Dilthey,* (cited in chap. 3, n. 5), chap. 4.

17. Goethe, "Einwirkung der neuern Philosophie," 50.

Part Three

Judgment and Reflective Interpretation

6

Ideas of the Imagination and Reflective Interpretation

In chapter 2 I characterized ideas of reason as rules for interpreting experience in relation to an overall scientific system. Whereas concepts of the understanding were said to establish rules for reading the manifold of sense in terms of objects in nature, ideas of reason were said to provide rules for interpreting these objects as part of a coherent and complete system of nature. In the reading of nature, the imagination had a semantical task in assigning the a priori categories of the understanding an objective meaning. However, the imagination had only a minimal role in reason's projection of the system of nature, for the interpretation of nature as a systematic whole primarily involved a regulative use of abstract ideas of reason.

By applying the reading metaphor of the *Critique of Pure Reason* to the syntheses of apprehension, reproduction, and recognition, we were able to account for the circularity of the Subjective Deduction. But because Kant's interpretation of nature in the first *Critique* was merely an extrapolation of reason from the reading of experience, it remained on the whole a one-directional abstract process not subject to the hermeneutic circle. The use of the ideas of reason to project the systematic unity of experience merely strives for the maximum possible degree of integration of the rules of the understanding. It directs "the understanding to a certain goal upon which the routes marked out by all its rules converge, as upon their point of intersection. This point is indeed a mere idea, a *focus imaginarius* . . . quite outside the bounds of experience" (*CI*, A644/B672). The *focus imaginarius* uses the imagination to extend the lines projected by the rules of the understanding, rather than to mediate between it and sense.

In the *Critique of Judgment* nature is no longer regarded as an abstract system in which all events can be explained by one mechanical type of causality. Once reflective judgment has specified nature into different species of beings, the interpretation of systematic order involves the articulation of nature into subsystems. To grasp their interrelations requires the mutual adjustment of parts and wholes characteristic of the hermeneutic circle. Here interpretation is subject to revision introduced by the imagination's efforts to link sense and intellect and becomes as much a function of judgment as of reason.

We have already seen that in reflective judgment the imagination proceeds from given particulars to educe a more general order from them. To account for the possibility of aesthetic apprehension, the categories were not applied mechanically, but specified reflectively. We can now take this a step further by supplementing Kant's conception of systematic interpretation with a conception of reflective interpretation. Whereas the former proceeds architectonically by striving for ever more encompassing wholes that eventually transcend our understanding, the latter proceeds tectonically by allowing the parts of a given whole to enrich and revise our initial understanding of it.

The potential for a theory of reflective interpretation can be explored by developing a set of ideas that are introduced in the *Critique of Judgment*. These are the normal, aesthetic, and teleological ideas, which are not rigidly prescribed by reason but are adaptive to the content of their subject matter. They provide no a priori determinant rules for interpretation, but indeterminate guidelines. Whereas rational ideas were directed at the overall system of nature, these new ideas can also be related to the more concrete level of the subsystems of nature. These ideas are used to discern order and meaning in aspects of experience left contingent by the laws of the understanding. What distinguishes a reflective interpretation of the particulars of experience from purely theoretical explanations using concepts and from dialectical reconstructions on the basis of rational ideas is that such an interpretation will "never analyze the structure of its object to the point of eliminating all contingency."[1]

Reflective interpretation is hermeneutical because, to paraphrase Jürgen Habermas, it apprehends *meaning* relations as relations of *fact*.[2] It might seem anachronistic to relate Kant's analysis of reflective judgment to language used by Habermas to characterize the hermeneutics of facticity of Dilthey and Heidegger where the concern is to understand the individuality and historicity of the particulars of

1. Jürgen Habermas, *Knowledge and Human Interests* (Boston: Beacon Press, 1971), 161.
2. See Habermas, *Knowledge,* 162.

experience.[3] But as I will attempt to show in the next chapter, it is precisely this coordination of particularity and universality that makes a historical event like the French Revolution worthy of interpretation for Kant. A contingent historical fact can intimate a necessary human telos. The coordination of contingency and necessity is also found in judgments concerning aesthetic purposiveness and in estimating what is normal.

An examination of the ideas introduced in the *Critique of Judgment* will lead us to supplement some of the analyses of earlier chapters. Normal ideas allow us to evaluate the members of a particular natural species relative to each other. Thus the discussion of normal ideas can provide more insight into the imagination's role in the reflective specification of nature (see chapter 3). In the analysis of the sublime (chapter 4), we saw the imagination restricted to a negative presentation of the moral ideas of reason, but now it can be shown that through aesthetic ideas the imagination can create positive, albeit indirect, presentations of rational ideas.

In this chapter I will focus on normal and aesthetic ideas, and the symbolic power of the poetic imagination. The next chapter will use teleological ideas to bring out moral interpretations of the world implicit in Kant's theories of history, culture, and religion. In the final chapter we will consider the idea of common sense as a presupposition of reflective interpretation.

Imagination and Normal Ideas

In the first two *Critiques* ideas were always products of reason, and Kant reasserts in the third *Critique* that an "idea properly means a rational concept" (*C3*, §17, 69). Nevertheless, he goes on to discuss normal and aesthetic ideas as products of the imagination. The term "normal idea" is introduced in section 17. The discussion of normal ideas is important as the first instance in which the imagination is allowed to present ideas, but it has been largely ignored. Most commentators have focused instead on the later sections devoted to aesthetic ideas and genius. This may be due to the fact that Kant's

---

3. The term "Faktizität" occurs in the writings of both Dilthey and Heidegger. In 1923 Heidegger subtitled his lectures on ontology "Hermeneutik der Faktizität."

claims about the normal idea occur as part of the analysis of the ideal of beauty and are not clearly formulated. He raises the question whether we arrive at the ideal of beauty empirically or a priori, but comes to no definite conclusion. The ideal of beauty has two components, the normal idea and the rational idea. The rational idea is purely a priori, but the normal idea seems to also exhibit some empirical elements that are left contingent. While the apparently hybrid status of the normal idea is unsatisfactory from the standpoint of explanation, it is suggestive for the theory of interpretation, which is neither purely empirical nor purely a priori.

Unlike the later aesthetic ideas, which are tied to supersensible or rational ideas, what Kant calls "the aesthetical *normal idea*" (*C3*, §17, 70) is more directly related to ordinary experience. It serves as a standard for judging an individual to be a member of a particular species. In its simplest form the normal idea may be understood as a mathematical average derived from experience. This is indicated by Kant's statements that the normal idea of the figure of a particular species "must take its elements from experience" (*C3*, §17, 70) and that the proportions of the average figure can be calculated "mechanically" (*C3*, §17, 71). However, the normal idea can also be arrived at through an aesthetical estimate of the imagination. This *aesthetical* normal idea adds an a priori moment in that it projects the purposiveness of the species. Such purposiveness "lies merely in the idea of the judging [subject]" (*C3*, §17, 70), and reflects "the image which is as it were designedly at the basis of nature's technique" (*C3*, §17, 70) in producing the species as a whole.

The *aesthetical* normal idea is an individual intuition of the imagination that is not given in any empirical intuition, nor is it simply a priori. The imagination produces this idea "by means of a dynamical effect," which arises from its "multiple apprehension" (*C3*, §17, 71; V, 234) of different figures.

Kant's description of the process of how the imagination generates such an aesthetic intuition or image represents another departure from the linear, serial model of inner sense of the first *Critique*, for in making its estimate of what is normal, the imagination allows images to be superimposed on each other. He writes: "If the mind is concerned with comparisons, the imagination can, in all probability, although not fully consciously, allow one image to fall on another (*ein*

Bild gleichsam auf das andere fallen zu lassen); and thus by the congruence of several of the same kind, come by an average which serves as the common measure of all" (*C3,* §17, 70; V, 234).[4] The normal figure arrived at through the imagination's aesthetic estimate is an average in the sense of being typical and as a common measure it may "contain nothing specifically characteristic" (*C3,* §17, 72).

Here Kant picks up again on the possibility of the simultaneous presentation of images suggested in his earlier discussion of synoptic image formation, or *Abbildung.* But while the *Abbilder* of chapter 1 brought together separate empirical images, the aesthetical normal idea represents another instance of the way in which the imagination can be said to read between the lines of ordinary experience. This idea is "the image for the whole race, which hovers between (*zwischen schwebende*) the variously different intuitions of individuals, which nature takes as archetype in her productions of the same species, but which appears not to be fully reached in any individual case" (*C3,* §17, 71; V, 234f).

The products of the imagination had been described in similar terms in the first *Critique,* where "each is a kind of monogram" (*C1,* A570/B598), that is, "a sketch or outline that hovers in the midst of (*im Mittel . . . schwebende*) various experiences" (*C1,* A570/B598; III, 385). In fact the aesthetic normal idea is comparable to the mathematical monogram of pure sensible concepts insofar as both involve a rule for the construction of a figure and are not reducible to a particular empirical image. However, their differences are indicative of how the mediating functions of the imagination are revised in moving from the reading of experience to its reflective interpretation. As a schema of the imagination, the monogram of a triangle is a rule for the purely a priori determination of any three-sided figure in space. The aesthetical normal idea "is not derived from proportions gotten from experience *as definite rules,* but in accordance with it rules for judging become in the first instance possible" (*C3,* §17, 71). This ambiguous

4. The language of similar images falling on each other (*aufeinander fallen*) represents the influence of Johann Nicolas Tetens, for it is literally that used by Tetens in describing one of the modes of imagination. See Tetens, *Philosophische Versuche über die menschliche Natur und ihre Entwicklung,* vol. 1 (1777), in *Neudrücke der Kant-Gesellschaft* (Berlin: Verlag von Reuther und Reichard, 1913), vol. 4, 103. For an overview of Tetens' three levels of the imagination, see James Engell, *The Creative Imagination: Enlightenment to Romanticism* (Cambridge: Harvard University Press, 1981), 118–28.

statement can be taken to mean that the normal idea is indeterminate in two ways: (1) it is not wholly determined by experience (or for that matter by any concept), and (2) the idea itself does not prescribe any definite rules.

The mathematical monogram, being a rule that makes it possible for us to generate a priori figures, is legislative in imposing its mathematical formal structures on nature. The aesthetical normal idea by contrast provides the rule for judging whether an empirical figure accords with the archetype used by nature in producing its species; it is interpretive since we cannot directly know the archetype of nature at the basis of an empirical form. Such an archetype is construed as an ideal that can be approximated only by means of the normal idea. Here the imagination plays a significant, new role in mediating between an idea and an ideal. This can be seen by comparing Kant's discussions of ideals in the first and third *Critiques*.

Concerning ideals of reason Kant writes in the *Critique of Pure Reason:* "As the idea gives the *rule,* so the ideal . . . serves as the *archetype* (*Urbild*) for the complete determination of the copy" (*C1,* A569/B597; III, 384). The ideal is archetypal in that it represents an idea of reason in its most perfect form. An ideal is an individual object completely adequate to an idea. Thus the Stoic ideal of a wise man would be in complete conformity with the ideas of virtue and wisdom. However, such a perfect individual can exist only in thought; ideals cannot be adequately realized in sense, whether through experience or imagination.

Kant stresses that the products of the imagination are of "an entirely different nature" (*C1,* A570/B598) from the ideal of reason. Since the imagination cannot do justice to the completeness of ideas of reason, any attempts by poets "to depict the [character of the perfectly] wise man in a romance, is impracticable" (*C1,* A570/B598). The products of the imagination "may be entitled, though improperly, ideals of sensibility inasmuch as they are viewed as being models (*Muster*) (not indeed realisable) of possible empirical intuitions, and yet furnish no rules that allow of being explained and examined" (*C1,* A570–71/B598–99; III, 385). These ideals of sensibility or models that artists "profess to carry in their heads" are dismissed by Kant as "incommunicable shadowy images" (*C1,* A570/B598).

In the reflective context of the *Critique of Judgment* Kant gives a more positive account of the imagination's role in the presentation of ideals. Indeed, the ideal of beauty is identified as an "ideal of the imagination" (*C3*, §17, 69), because it is based on an individual presentation rather than on concepts. Kant claims that the aesthetic normal idea, as one of the components of the ideal of beauty, can be completely presented *in concreto* in a model image (*Musterbild*)" (*C3*, §17, 70; V, 233). The model produced by the imagination is no longer dismissed as "shadowy" and "incommunicable"; it is a concrete image that can be presented as a common measure.

In the analysis of the imagination's ideal of beauty, model and archetype are no longer sharply distinguished, as they were in the case of the ideal of reason. Thus Kant describes the archetype of taste as "the highest model" (*C3*, §17, 68). This is in keeping with the judgment of taste, which relies, not on a priori determinate rules, but on given models that play an exemplary role. No such model can have more than a temporary guiding function, for ultimately everyone must produce the model of taste in himself.

Whereas the ideal of reason is a completely determinate archetype, the ideal of the imagination contains a model image that makes possible reflection about an archetype. The model image of the aesthetical normal idea represents a norm for judging what is typical and can give only a provisional estimate of nature's archetype. It serves as the rule for the correct presentation of the form of the species. However, this is but the minimal condition that must be satisfied for a thing to be beautiful.

The ideal of beauty also contains a rational idea that projects a maximum standard of perfection. According to Kant the ideal of perfection pertains only to things whose purpose can be fully determined conceptually. Such determination is not possible for most beautiful objects, such as flowers. In fact, Kant claims that the ideal of beauty applies to the human species alone, for the "only being which has the purpose of its existence in itself is man, who can determine his purpose by reason" (*C3*, §17, 69). The rational idea of man's purpose is a moral idea and provides the ideal of human beauty an objective universality that transcends the subjective universality of the pure aesthetic judgment. The normal idea of human beauty, being an interpretive or reflective idea adaptive to particular experience, is not yet universal. Although it may contain "nothing specifically characteristic" (*C3*, §17, 72), its concrete presentation in a model image will vary according to empirical differences among communities. Thus

Kant claims that the Chinese and the Europeans "must have a different normal idea of the beauty of the [human figure]" (*C3*, §17, 71). These contingent differences need not contravene the objective universality of the ideal, for different aesthetic normal ideas of human beauty are merely provisional attempts to estimate a universal archetype through typical model images. The ideal itself, Kant writes, "consists in the expression of the *moral,* without which the object would not please universally and thus positively (not merely negatively in the accurate presentation)" (*C3*, §17, 72).

Only in the case of human beauty does perfection have aesthetic relevance. In Kant's view, the common eighteenth-century definition of beauty as a sensible mode of perfection is inadequate, because it makes aesthetic consciousness a cognitive or moral mode of experience. For Kant beauty provides a pure aesthetic pleasure which has its own transcendental justification apart from our cognitive and moral interests. It is therefore characterized as disinterested and purposive without a purpose. Yet the fact that aesthetic *consciousness* in its purity is neither cognitive nor moral does not mean that we do not often have aesthetic *experiences* into which cognitive and moral considerations also enter. The discussions of the ideal of beauty show Kant supplementing his transcendental analysis of the pure aesthetic consciousness of the "free beauty" of a flower with an account of the "dependent beauty" of the human figure that is determined by a rational concept (see *C3*, §16, for Kant's distinction between free and dependent beauty).

Aesthetic Ideas

With the aesthetic idea the interrelation of the imagination and reason is carried a step further. In the ideal of beauty we saw the normal idea of the imagination work in conjunction with a rational idea. The aesthetic idea, however, is claimed to be the "counterpart (pendant)" (*C3*, §49, 157) of a rational idea as the imagination assumes a role complementary to that of reason in striving to complete our experience. This is most fully displayed in the poetic imagination.

> The poet ventures to realize to sense, rational ideas of invisible beings, the kingdom of the blessed, hell, eternity, creation, etc., or even if he deals with things of which there

are examples in experience, e.g., death, envy and all vices, also love, fame and the like—he tries by means of imagination, which emulates the play of reason in its quest after a maximum, to go beyond the limits of experience and to present them to sense with a completeness of which there is no example in nature. This is properly speaking the art of the poet, in which the faculty of aesthetical ideas can manifest itself in its entire strength. (*C3*, §49, 157–58)

Striving after a maximum is not limited to the art of poetry (*Dichtkunst*); what Kant elsewhere calls the *Dichtungstrieb* (poetic drive) may be applied to the painter, the architect, and composer, as well as to the metaphysician (see *RA*, 1485; XV, 701, 703; 1775–77). The poetic drive to completion displayed by the imagination, now conceived as "the faculty of presenting *aesthetical ideas*" (*C3*, §49, 157), can also be related back to *Ausbildung* or what was called "completing formation" in chapter 1.

Both rational and aesthetic ideas go beyond the limits of experience and they fail to produce determinate knowledge of empirical objects. However, they differ in the way they preclude the normal syntheses of sensible intuitions and concepts of the understanding that Kant requires for experience. A rational idea involves a transcendent "concept (of the supersensible) corresponding to which an intuition can never be given" (*C3*, §57, 187). An aesthetic idea is "an *intuition* (of the imagination) for which an adequate concept can never be found" (*C3*, §57, 187). Here there is an excess on the side of what Kant calls "the full inner intuition of the imagination" (*C3*, §57, 189; V, 343) for which the understanding cannot find a determinate concept.

In what way the imagination can present more material than can be comprehended in a concept is shown in section 49, on genius. There Kant writes, "The imagination . . . is very powerful in the creation (*Schaffung*) of another nature, as it were, out of the material that actual nature gives it" (*C3*, §49, 157; V, 314).

As I pointed out in chapter 1, Kant had denied the possibility of a radically creative imagination that could produce images whose content is not dependent on the senses. This point is reiterated in the *Anthropology*, where he writes: "No matter how great an artist, and even enchantress, imagination might be, it is still not creative (*schöpferisch*), but must get the material for its images from the *senses*" (*AP*, §28, 45; VII, 168). However, the claim for creativity in the *Critique of*

Judgment is not essentially inconsistent with these other statements, for the imagination is still seen to be working with the material supplied by nature. The creativity now attributed to the imagination does not refer to the creation ex nihilo of sensuous images. In the *Critique of Pure Reason* Kant had already described the imagination as creative in the mathematical construction of purely formal figures. Concerning the a priori intuition of the imagination, he wrote that "we create (*schaffen*) for ourselves, in space and time, through a uniform synthesis, the objects themselves—these objects being viewed simply as quanta" (*C1*, A723/B751).

The creation involved in aesthetic ideas is not an *Urbildung*, or original formation, but a kind of *Umbildung*, or transformative process. Through the creation of another nature by the imagination, "we transform (*bilden um*) experience" (*C3*, §49, 157; V, 314) according to analogical laws and the higher principles of reason. In the process of transformation the imagination is freed from the law of association "so that the material supplied to us by nature in accordance with this law can be worked up into something different which surpasses (*übertrifft*) nature" (*C3*, §49, 157; V, 314).

Kant's use of the term "surpass" points to a significant difference in the way rational and aesthetic ideas may be said to go "beyond" the limits of experience. Rational ideas transcend nature, and aesthetic ideas surpass it by transforming and enriching experience. While reason seeks the completion of nature in a supersensible realm, the imagination attains a completion that remains tied to the sensible realm itself. The imagination either finds a sensible presentation of a transcendent idea of reason, or gives a more complete presentation than is found in nature of such experienced things as death, envy, and love.

This creative power of the imagination is exhibited by genius, which Kant calls the "faculty of aesthetic ideas" (*C3*, §57, 189). Whereas in ordinary experience the understanding provides the rules to the imagination, genius is characterized by a special proportion of the imagination and the understanding that allows the former to suggest rules to the latter. Kant writes: "In an aesthetic point of view it [the imagination] is free to furnish unsought, over and above that agreement with a concept, abundance of undeveloped material for the understanding, to which the understanding paid no regard in its concept but which it applies, though not objectively for cognition, yet subjectively for the enlivening (*Belebung*) of the cognitive powers and therefore also indirectly to cognitions" (*C3*, §47, 160; V, 316–17). This abundance of undeveloped material associated with a concept is the intuitive content that can no longer be subsumed under the concept and points beyond it to become an aesthetic idea. By allowing the imagination "to spread itself over a number of kindred representations" (*C3*, §49, 158), the aesthetic idea leads us to think about the concept's "relationship to other concepts" (*C3*, §49, 158). Although Kant says that aesthetic ideas enlarge our given concepts, they are suggestive in a way that shows the limits of these concepts. The aesthetic idea is claimed to occasion "much thinking" (*denken*), without however, any one definite thought (*Gedanke*), i.e., any *concept,* being capable of being adequate to it" (*C3*, §49, 157; V, 314). Thought, which is a function of reason, is here occasioned by an excess of intuitive content that cannot be contained within the concepts of the understanding.

Kant illustrates how an aesthetic idea represents a rational idea through the image of Jupiter as an eagle with lightning in its claws. Such imagery provides only "approximate representations" (*C3*, §49, 158) that are not strictly subsumable under the rational idea of a god. They display what Kant calls "aesthetical attributes of the object, which accompany the logical and stimulate the imagination" (*C3*, §49, 159). Such aesthetic attributes of a god can only indirectly represent his power and majesty. Similarly, the representation of the end of a pleasant summer day offers only an aesthetic attribute for the rational idea of the proper attitude toward the end of one's life. Yet these aesthetic attributes help to enliven what would otherwise be mere abstract rational ideas, i.e., make them meaningful in relation to experience.

Just as normal ideas were interpretive in approximating the archetypes of natural species, so aesthetic ideas are interpretive in approximating rational ideas. Aesthetic ideas allow us to integrate our experience in ways left contingent by the abstract system of nature based on the understanding and elaborated by reason. They draw out, in Kant's words, "a concept's implications (*Folgen*) and its kinship with other concepts" (*C3*, §49, 158; V, 315; Pluhar, 183). Thereby aesthetic ideas can be said to contribute to the process of reflective interpretation that suggests significant affinities even where direct conceptual connections cannot be demonstrated. Although such ideas cannot enlarge concepts qua concepts, they broaden our interpretation of experience by presenting rational ideas to sense. In particular, aesthetic ideas can add a moral dimension to the meaning of experience. These potential interpretive functions can be brought out by relating the expression of aesthetic ideas to the symbolic presentation of moral ideas of reason.

Expression and Symbolic Presentation

Although aesthetic ideas occasion much thinking, they are, strictly speaking, ineffable. There is no assurance that the special proportions of the mental faculties characteristic of genius can be related to the normal proportion necessary for intersubjective knowledge. Thus the originality of genius in producing aesthetic ideas must be matched with a power to communicate them. For this, genius requires a special talent that Kant calls "spirit."

Spirit was defined in the previous chapter as the enlivening principle of the mind that unifies in terms of an overarching idea. But in relation to genius, spirit is the "talent" for giving concrete expression to aesthetic ideas so that the life of the mind can be shared.[5] Through spirit, genius is able "to express the ineffable state of mind implied by a certain representation and to make it universally communicable—whether the expression be in speech or painting or statuary" (*C3*, §49, 161).

Kant claims that in expressing an aesthetic idea, spirit must "apprehend (*auffassen*) the quickly passing play of the imagination and unify it into a concept" (*C3*, §49, 161; V, 317). This is an "original" concept that can be communicated without rules while disclosing a new rule (*C3*, §49, 161). It may seem inconsistent for Kant to say that a new concept is required to express an aesthetic idea since, by definition, an aesthetic idea can have no concept adequate to it. But the concept in question is subsequently explained to be the concept that the artist must have of his work of art as a purpose. Concepts are thus not needed for expressing the idea as such, but only insofar as expression is part of a larger intentional artistic process that "presupposes a determinate concept of the product as a purpose" (*C3*, §49, 161; V, 317).

---

5. Here Kant anticipates, if only fleetingly, the whole tradition from Hegel through Dilthey that links spirit with various modes of objectification.

Kant's reference to a concept of the artistic object may have been meant to affirm the universal communicability of the expression. However, as we will see in chapter 8, one of the fundamental claims of the *Critique of Judgment* is that there is a *sensus communis* that allows us to communicate universally without appealing to concepts. Determinant communication through discursive concepts of the understanding is not always possible and must be supplemented by indeterminate modes of communication whether directly through feeling or indirectly through objective expressions.

We can gain a clearer idea of what is involved in the nondiscursive expression of aesthetic ideas by relating it to the symbolic function of the imagination. In emulating reason's striving after a maximum, the imagination functions as a mode of *Ausbildung* (completing formation), and produces an aesthetic idea that gives an intuitive approximation of the totality of reason. In expressing such an idea, the completing function of the imagination goes over into the process of analogue or symbolic formation (*Gegenbildung*) (see chapter 1). Here the intuitive counterpart (*Gegenstück*) of the rational idea is specified as its symbol or linguistic analogue (*Gegenbild: symbolum*) (RA 313a; XV, 123; 1769).

In section 59, "Beauty as the Symbol of Morality," the process whereby the imagination provides an intuition for an a priori concept is called "hypotyposis." There are two modes of hypotyposis, schematical and symbolic, which correspond to determinant application and reflective specification (see chapters 2 and 3). Schematical hypotyposis supplies a direct intuition for a pure concept of the understanding. Here the imagination produces an a priori temporal schema which can then be applied to particular objects of experience. Symbolic hypotyposis involves the presentation of a supersensible concept of reason, so that the intuition can be given only indirectly. It is a reflective specification in which the imagination relates reason to sense by means of formal analogies found through reflection on rational concepts and empirical intuitions. In symbolic presentation "judgment exercises a double function, first applying the concept to the object of a sensible intuition and then applying the mere rule of reflection made upon that intuition to a quite different object of which the first is only the symbol. Thus a monarchical state is represented by a living body if it is governed by national laws, and by a mere machine . . . if governed by an individual absolute will" (*C3*, §59, 197–98). One object can be a symbol for another if reflection can specify similar formal relations among their parts. Insofar as they both operate as self-regulating wholes, an empirical organism can be used as a symbol for reflecting on the "quite different object" of a law-governed state.

Kant stresses that symbols and schemata are intuitive presentations and must be contrasted with words or other sensible signs used for the simple expression of concepts. Words or sensible signs are "mere *characterizations* or designations" that accompany concepts. They "contain nothing belonging to the intuition of the object and only serve as a means for reproducing the concepts, according to the law of association of the imagination, and consequently in a subjective point of view" (*C3*, §59, 197). This use of words or linguistic expressions as external, accompanying signs works well enough in conjunction with the direct but nonlinguistic presentation of the object in schematical hypotyposis. However, language plays a more integral, intuitive role in the indirect symbolic presentation of ideas. We will be able to exemplify these two functions of language by examining what is involved in the schematical hypotyposis of Kant's *category* of substance on the one hand and the symbolic hypotyposis of Locke's *idea* of substance on the other hand.

In schematizing the logical meaning of a category, the objective meaning is produced by the imagination without the use of language. The process of determinant application establishes a direct semantical relation among Kant's category of substance, its temporal schema of permanence in time, and the possible objects to which it can be applied. Because the schema of the imagination already intuitively anticipates the scientifically meaningful attributes of the object, language need only designate these attributes without intuitively presenting them.

However, Locke's idea of substance possesses meanings that do not derive from the schematization of its logical categorial use. To the extent that substance is also an idea of reason that transcends the understanding, it can obtain an intuitive meaning only indirectly through the process of reflective specification. As Kant points out, "Our language is full of indirect presentations . . . in which the expression does not contain the proper schema for the concept, but merely a symbol for reflection. Thus the words . . . *substance* (as Locke expresses it, the support of accidents), and countless others are not schematical but symbolical hypotyposes and expressions for concepts, not by means of a direct intuition, but only by analogy with it" (C3, §59, 198). We can see that the empirical history of a word can itself provide clues for reflection on its meaning. Etymologically, the word "substance" means to stand under and presents an empirical analogue for the idea that something must support the qualities that we experience. Here language functions symbolically to allow us to indirectly intuit the idea of something we know not what. Similarly, the word "depend" is a symbolic expression differing from a mere sign because it contains an intuitive content indirectly derived from reflection on the empirical analogue of something being "held up from above" (C3, §59, 198).

Aesthetic Ideas and the "True Interpretation" of Beauty

Although aesthetic ideas are not mentioned in Kant's account of symbolic hypotyposis, they play an important intermediary role in linking beauty and morality. Kant's claim that beauty is a symbol of morality is commonly taken to mean that beautiful forms are the expressions rather than the presentations of moral ideas of reason. But this is to overlook Kant's earlier statement that all beauty is "the expression of aesthetical ideas" (C3, §51, 164). Beauty can serve as the symbolic presentation of a rational idea because it is also the expression of a mediating aesthetic idea.

It was shown in chapter 3 above that a beautiful form is apprehended not just as a perceptual shape, but as purposive; that is, beauty provides a hint or "trace" that nature is in general agreement with a principle of purposiveness. There we noted the theoretical purposiveness of beauty, but Kant also speaks of its moral purposiveness or significance. The "true interpretation (Auslegung)" of beauty in nature shows aesthetic feeling to be "akin to the moral feeling" (C3, §42, 143; V, 301). The trace of purposiveness found in beauty is apprehended "as if it were a lucky chance favoring our design" (C3, intro., v, 20). The harmony of the cognitive faculties that is felt when we contemplate a beautiful object is pleasurable at least partly because it is unexpected. From the standpoint of reflective judgment a systematic organization of our experience is necessary, but whenever we succeed in finding a specific instance of such integral order it is regarded "as merely contingent" (C3, intro., vi, 24).

The contingency or facticity of the beautiful form could be called a "fact of a priori feeling" just as Kant calls our consciousness of the fundamental moral law a "fact of reason" in the *Critique of Practical Reason* (*C2*, 31). This fact of reason cannot itself be rationally derived nor can it be given in an intuition. It has a paradoxical status because it is a datum that cannot be intuited either empirically or purely. If it were available to empirical intuition it could not be a fact of *reason*. Nor can it be given through pure intuition, because the sole kind of pure intuition available to humans is that which provides the source of mathematics. Since we are not capable of having an intellectual intuition of a moral fact of reason, it seems appropriate to conceive our access to it through the only other mode of receptivity available to us, namely, feeling. Indeed, at a later point in the *Critique of Practical Reason* Kant discusses our consciousness of the moral law in terms of our feeling of respect for it—a feeling which is not pathological or empirical, but purely the effect of an intellectual idea. The interpretation of the "sole fact of pure reason" (*C2*, 31) as a felt fact accessible through the "singular" (*C2*, 82) feeling of respect supports our efforts to relate aesthetic and moral ideas, and should be kept in mind when we consider the relation of teleological and practical judgments in the next chapter.

In the discussion of beauty as a symbol of morality Kant shows that we commonly attribute moral qualities to beautiful objects: "We call buildings or trees majestic . . . ; even colors are called innocent, modest, tender, because they excite feelings which have something analogous to the consciousness of the state of mind brought about by moral judgments" (*C3*, §59, 200; V, 354). Such morally tinged "aesthetic attributes" lead to the formation of aesthetic ideas which are the felt counterparts of moral ideas. It is these intermediary aesthetic ideas that are symbolically expressed in beautiful forms.

It may seem strange for Kant to claim that natural as well as artistic beauty involves the expression of aesthetic ideas. But Kant makes it clear that we are not thereby assigning aesthetic attributes to natural objects in a realistic sense, for aesthetic judgments function according to the principle of the idealism of purposiveness of both nature and art. Thus after asserting that "the song of birds proclaims joyfulness and contentment with existence," he adds, "at least so we interpret nature, whether it have this design or not" (*C3*, §42, 144–45; V, 302). To regard a bird's song as expressive of joy is not to make a determinant claim about any conscious design in nature, but to make a reflective judgment about a formal purposiveness of nature in relation to our own theoretical and practical ends. This means that the purposiveness in the beauty of nature is a product of interpretation. In judging natural beauty "the important point is not what nature is, or even, as a purpose, is in relation to us, *but how we take it*" (*C3*, §58, 195; emphasis added). The aesthetic idea provides a rule of interpretation that indirectly presents the moral attitude.

In the case of artistic beauty, the idealism of purposiveness is more obvious. Here the aesthetic idea is a product of genius through which, according to Kant, "nature gives the rule to art" (*C3*, §46, 150). The nature that gives the rule to art is not the external nature of the first *Critique,* but "nature in the subject" (*C3*, §46, 150). Whereas aesthetic ideas are produced by the natural disposition of a genius as an individual subject, their expression in beautiful art involves a "spirit" that reflects the purposiveness of human nature in general. In symbolizing morality, beauty elevates us beyond mere sensibility, and judgment "finds itself to be referred to something within the subject as well as without him, something which is neither nature nor freedom, but which yet is connected with the supersensible ground of the latter" (*C3*, §59, 199). This supersensible ground can be regarded as the "supersensible substrate of humanity" that points to the unity of the human subject in Kant's solution to the antinomy of taste (see *C3*, §57; and chapter 4). What ultimately allows beauty to serve as a symbolic link between the natural and the moral is the idea of humanity.

The expression of aesthetic ideas through symbolic presentation helps to focus reflection and specify given concepts of reason. We can show the mediating role of aesthetic ideas in reflective specification by returning to Kant's example of the republican state being symbolized by the living body. At first sight, the republican or law-governed state may appear to present a rational idea. However, I regard it as a politically applied aesthetic idea that mediates between the teleological idea of an empirical organism and the rational idea of a supersensible or divine kingdom of ends. The governing principle of all three ideas is that they are systems displaying an immanent purposiveness characterized by a mutual adaptation of the parts of a whole. The significance of an aesthetic idea lies in its power to establish an imaginative cross-referencing between different levels of system. It allows us to specify the abstract rules for interpreting the meaning of an absolute system such as the kingdom of ends in terms of more limited systems such as an empirical organism and an imagined ideal of government. The symbol of a living body expresses the aesthetic idea of a law-governed, republican state and as such provides an intuitive analogue for reflectively specifying the moral idea of the kingdom of ends.

The process of reflective specification which was earlier applied to the system of nature (see chapter 3) can now be extended to the practical aims of reason as well. In addition to ordering nature into a set of subsystems, reflection can also focus moral ideas by means of symbolic analogues. Rational ideas inspire the thought involved in aesthetic ideas, and in turn the symbolic presentation of this thought helps to specify these rational ideas. The expression of an aesthetic idea does not necessarily produce a new concept, but it can supply a symbolic analogue whereby the traditional concepts of reason are adapted to the particular subdomains of experience.

Instead of the abstract interpretation of systematic order determined by rational ideas, a reflective mode of interpretation uses normal and aesthetic ideas to articulate a more concrete order at the level of experience. The normal idea interprets nature's archetype by means of a model image that embodies what is typical in a way that can be commonly understood. Such model images are comparable to Diltheyan and Weberian types in providing indeterminate rules or norms for judging particulars. Even the manner in which actual experience departs from the typical is heuristic in suggesting scientific explanations of the concrete order of nature. The expression of aesthetic ideas in terms of symbolic presentation is typical in a more limited sense characteristic of art. Yet even these lower or hypo-types expressed in works of art can lead those appreciative of them to develop their own ways of specifying the significance of experience. Just as every work of art should be more than an ectype, or passive copy, of an archetypal order, so everyone is responsible for developing within himself the highest model of taste.

We have now seen the imagination described both as a faculty of producing and reproducing representations (*Vorstellungen*) and as a faculty of creating presentations (*Darstellungen*). Its power to represent (*vorstellen*) is primarily a perceptual function. Thus in the first *Critique* the imagination was defined as the power to intuit an object even without its presence (see chapter 2). Because the imagination can relate what is present to what is absent, it could be called an indirect mode of seeing. The imagination's ability to present (*darstellen*) is also intuitive, but is more than perceptual. To present is to exhibit the meaning of something. The schemata of the first *Critique* were direct modes of presenting the categories of the understanding to make them applicable to the particulars of sense. They were viewed as semantical rules that give the categories an objective, referential meaning. The symbolic mode of presentation introduced in the third *Critique* adds a nonreferential type of meaning that we call significance. Symbolic presentations are indirect modes of expressing certain ideas that cannot be directly articulated by means of concepts.

To the extent that the imagination has a role to play in the symbolic mode of presenting rational ideas through aesthetic ideas, it can be said to be doubly indirect. The imagination must not only supplement with mental images what it cannot directly perceive, but also it must use indirect interpretive strategies to compensate for what it cannot directly understand through the conventional reading of experience. Whereas schemata make possible a determinant reading of nature, symbolic presentations allow us to arrive at a reflective interpretation of things that surpass nature.

As we saw in chapter 5, the symbol of a living mind can enliven our rational idea of God and ensure that we do not lapse into abstract deism. The capacity of the imagination to provide symbolic knowledge of God does not shatter the critical framework of the first *Critique,* for it does not claim to produce any determinate knowledge of anything transcending experience. It merely enlivens our indeterminate thoughts about the overall scheme of things and guides reflection on meaning by creating indirect analogies with experience. Whereas the regulative use of rational ideas of the first *Critique* was used for the systematic integration of the world on the phenomenal plane, the reflective use of rational ideas through aesthetic ideas can produce an interpretation of reality that encompasses the various levels of our awareness. The criterion of the imagination in this context is an enlivened presentation which captures the felt completeness and balance of life.

7
Teleological Ideas and the Authentic Interpretation of History

Aesthetic purposiveness has been explored as a general idea for finding significance in life. In the Critique of Teleological Judgment, Kant no longer speaks of purposiveness without a purpose. Instead, he specifies the idea of the purposiveness of nature by showing that certain natural processes can be fully understood only if in addition to being explained by mechanical causation, they are described in terms of purposes. Through the idea of a natural purpose, determinant explanations of organisms on the basis of theoretical reason are supplemented with reflective judgments concerning their ends. In chapter 5 we spoke primarily of the immanent purposiveness of individual organisms, but it was noted that questions concerning the external purposiveness or usefulness of one species of life to another could not be resolved without knowledge of a final purpose. This means that in the last analysis the problem of teleology is not only theoretical, but also practical.

From a theoretical perspective man can be considered simply as part of a chain of natural purposes. Kant concedes that man may even be regarded as a means, as Linnaeus claims, serving to preserve "a certain equilibrium between the producing and the destructive powers of nature" (C3, §82, 276–77). Man does appear to be superior to other living creatures in that he has the capacity to use them all for his ends. But Kant stresses that he is not distinguished from other creatures by being destined to achieve the natural end of happiness. Noting that man is not safe from the devastations of nature, Kant writes that she "has not taken him for her special darling and favored him with benefit above all animals" (C3, §83, 280).

It is only by adding the practical perspective that human purposiveness can be fully defined in relation to the purposiveness of nature. As set forth in Kant's moral writings, man is an end in himself and as such a final purpose independent of nature. This moral idea of a final purpose must be related to the teleological idea of man as a natural purpose in order to establish the framework for interpreting human history.

Although Kant does not thematize the problem of history in the *Critique of Judgment,* his discussion there of teleology and culture provides a basis for a reflective interpretation of history. If aesthetic ideas point to the possibility that nature may be in harmony with morality, teleological ideas in reflective interpretation provide the means for conceptualizing how nature and morality can be reconciled in human history. Before exploring these applications of Kant's reflective approach to teleology, I will consider two earlier essays that deal with history without the use of reflective judgment. The first of these essays still involves a speculative use of teleology; the second a mere imaginary, conjectural use.

A Teleological Interpretation of Nature and History

In his essay "Idea for a Universal History from a Cosmopolitan Point of View," published in 1784, Kant explores the possibility of discerning an overall order in history. Although man possesses a noumenal freedom, his actions are phenomenal events determined by universal laws which may be discerned by regarding history from the point of view of the human race as a whole. "Since the philosopher cannot presuppose any [conscious] individual purpose among men in their great drama," Kant writes, "there is no other expedient for him except to try to see if he can discover a natural purpose in this idiotic course of things human."[1] Viewing history as an extension of nature, he interprets the overall order of history in terms of the teleology of nature. This is not the nature we have discussed before, but a Nature—also called Providence (see *UH,* 25)—that has a plan for man's development which will make possible the attainment of his moral end. More specifically, the history of mankind is to be interpreted as the realization of a "secret plan" to establish (1) "a perfectly constituted state, as the only condition in which the capacities of mankind can be fully developed" (*UH,* 21), and (2) a world federation that will ensure just and peaceful relations among states. Our past and present suffering can be seen as

---

1. Kant, "Idea for a Universal History from a Cosmopolitan Point of View" (hereafter *UH*), trans. Lewis White Beck, in *Kant on History,* ed. L. W. Beck (Indianapolis: Bobbs-Merrill, 1963), 12.

Nature's means to spur man to improve himself. Kant claims: "Man wishes concord; but Nature knows better what is good for the race; she wills discord . . . [to] drive men to new exertions of their forces and thus to the manifold development of their capacities" (*UH*, 16).

Kant's language makes it appear that man's development, rather than being a product of his own reason or will, is the unwitting result of a telos of Nature that uses his passions. Although Kant also states that "humankind should itself achieve this goal" (*UH*, 16) of a universal civil society, the basic perspective is one in which Nature's determination or will is dominant. Thus he speaks of the cosmopolitan society as "Nature's highest intention (*höchsten Absicht*)" (*UH*, 23; VIII, 28). This has been translated as "ultimate purpose," but in this essay written before the third *Critique*, the teleological idea of Nature's "highest intention" differs from that of an "ultimate purpose" in not being used reflectively.

Kant acknowledges that his projection of history "in accordance with an Idea of how the course of the world must be if it is to lead to certain rational ends" (*UH*, 24) may seem to be nothing more than a historical romance. However, he contends that the idea is nonetheless useful as a "guiding thread for presenting as a system" (*UH*, 24) the otherwise confused course of history. Kant declares that he has no intention of displacing empirical history, and is only suggesting another point of view. What he is proposing in effect with his idea of a universal history is a speculative interpretation seeking an overall moral meaning in empirical history. Kant's moral perspective is typical of the Enlightenment in seeing human development as the refinement of a "coarse, natural disposition for ethical (*sittlichen*) discrimination into definite practical principles" and as the transformation of society "into a moral (*moralische*) whole" (*UH*, 15; VIII, 21).

According to Kant, the study of civic constitutions from the time of the Greeks will reveal a regular progress that accords with his "a priori guiding thread (*Leitfaden*)" (*UH*, 25; VIII, 30).[2] Instead of placing all our hope for a rational end in another world, Kant's history from a cosmopolitan point of view projects a future condition "in which the destiny of the race can be fulfilled here on earth" (*UH*, 25). The cosmopolitan idea appealed to in this essay may not point to an-

---

2. In this passage *Leitfaden* is somewhat misleadingly rendered as "principle" in the English translation.

other world, but its use of teleology is not yet reflective. It is still very much a rational idea that is brought down to earth by being used pragmatically: "The Idea can help, though only from afar, to bring the millennium to pass" (*UH*, 22).

Universal History and the Development of Freedom

In the "Idea for a Universal History" the history of mankind was viewed primarily from the perspective of a providential plan, but the "Conjectural Beginning of Human History," published two years later in 1786, focuses more on the role of man's reason in his moral development. Viewing the beginning of human history in terms of man's emergence from "the tutelage of nature,"[3] Kant attempts "a historical account of the first development of freedom from its original predisposition in human nature" (*CB*, 53).

Kant limits his claims from the start by characterizing his venture into conjectural history as "a mere pleasure trip" (*CB*, 54) and an "exercise of the imagination guided by reason" (*CB*, 53). While the empirical historian may use his imagination only sparingly to interpolate or "fill gaps in the record" (*CB*, 53), the philosophical historian may also use his imagination to extrapolate or go beyond the record by following "a guiding thread (*Leitfaden*) rationally derived from experience" (*CB*, 54; VIII, 110). Although Kant's conjectural account of the beginning of human history makes use of the imagination, it should not be fictional or arbitrarily invented (*erdichtet*) (*CB*, 53; VIII, 109). It can rely on experience, "if only one presupposes that human actions were in the beginning no better and no worse than we find them now" (*CB*, 53; VIII, 109).

Kant distinguishes four steps in the use of reason which are at the basis of man's social and moral development. The account begins with human beings in a "state of servitude" (*CB*, 56), that is, ruled by the natural instincts obeyed by all animals. The first stirrings of reason loosen instinctual ties by instituting comparisons that lead beyond instinctual knowledge. Reason aided by the imagination creates alternatives and becomes recognized as the power of choice. In the first

3. Kant, "Conjectural Beginning of Human History" (hereafter *CB*), trans. Emil Fackenheim, in *Kant on History*, ed. Lewis White Beck, 53–68 (Indianapolis: Bobbs-Merrill, 1963), 60.

stage, man "discovered in himself a power of choosing for himself a way of life, of not being bound without alternative to a single way, like the animals" (*CB,* 56). Human reason gains its first taste of freedom, which in Kant's teleological interpretation of history is to be fully achieved in the cosmopolitan society.

In the second phase of its development, reason shows its mastery over the impulses. By means of the imagination, sexual instinct becomes more than the satisfaction of animal desire. Inclinations originally directed at objects of the senses are rendered "more inward (*inniglich*) and constant" (*CB,* 57), and controlled by reason. "*Refusal* was the feat which brought about the passage from merely sensual (*empfundenen*) to spiritual (*idealistischen*) attractions, from mere animal desire gradually to love, and along with this from the feeling of the merely agreeable to a taste for beauty" (*CB,* 57). Kant remarks that we also have a first hint of man's development as an ethical (*sittliches*) creature in the emergence of a sense of decency (*Sittsamkeit*) or the inclination to gain respect through manners.

The conscious expectation of the future is the third step taken by reason. According to Kant, this is "the most decisive mark of the human's advantage" (*CB,* 58), for instead of being absorbed by what happens in the present, he is able to prepare himself for distant ends. Man learns to improve his situation by planning ahead, but at the same time he is introduced to cares and troubles, including the awareness of his eventual death.

The fourth step taken by reason gives man the initial dim comprehension that he is truly the end of nature. This raises man above all animals, which are no longer viewed as fellow creatures but as means or tools for his ends. At the same time, every human being is placed in a relation of equality with all rational beings and cannot be treated as a mere means. By making man an end in himself, this last step of reason effects "man's *release* from the womb of nature" (*CB,* 59).

The account of man's transition from his "merely animal condition to the state of humanity" (*C3,* 60) is correlated with the biblical story of man's fall and expulsion from the garden of Eden. Kant inserts references to specific passages in Genesis and occasionally makes allusions to its language and imagery. However, the scriptures are approached, not primarily as a historical document or text to be interpreted, but only as a "map" (*CB,* 54) for his own philosophical construction of the beginning of human history. It is not until after the writing of the *Critique of Judgment* that Kant addresses the problem of interpretation in relation to religious texts. Here Kant is only attempting to show that his conceptual narrative of the growth of reason concurs with the "route sketched out" (*CB*, 54) in Genesis 2–6.

The conclusion drawn from Kant's Enlightenment perspective departs from traditional Christianity in minimizing the doctrine of original sin. Kant acknowledges that in being driven from the security or "garden" of childhood, man is exposed to danger and suffering. But man should not blame these "evils (*Übeln*)" on Providence, nor "attribute his own offense to an original sin committed by his first parents. For free actions can in no aspects be hereditary" (*CB*, 68). Kant concludes that the "first use of reason" in going against the advice of nature is always an "abuse" (*CB*, 68) of reason—this is as much the case ontogenetically as phylogenetically. Man's release from the womb of nature may be regarded as unfortunate by individual men concerned with happiness, but it must be regarded as good for man as a species. We may wish to look back on the state of nature as a blissful paradise, but this is only an illusory creation of the imagination. Instead, reason should impel us to develop all our capacities and progress toward our perfection. Here Kant exhibits a moral distrust of the imagination as being primarily concerned with happiness—a distrust also evident in the *Critique of Practical Reason*, as we will see later.

Kant distinguishes two kinds of history in the "Conjectural Beginning": a history of nature that "begins with the good, for it is the work of God" and a history of freedom that "begins with evil (*vom Bösen*), for it is the work of man" (*CB*, 60; VIII, 115). However, the relation between these two kinds of history is not clear because of Kant's varied use of the term "nature." The growth of reason in the beginning of human history entails a control over nature as identified with animal instincts and sensual gratification. But nature is also seen as the providential source or power establishing man as both an animal and a moral species. Nature, Kant writes, "has given us two different dispositions for two different purposes, the one for man as an animal species (*Thiergattung*), the other for him as an ethical species (*sittlicher Gattung*)" (*CB*, 61–62n; VIII, 117n). This broader sense of nature continues the teleological interpretation set forth in the "Idea for a Universal History," where man's moral development was claimed to be the purpose of a providential Nature. With nature interpreted broadly as the source of our animal and ethical dispositions, the history of nature can itself encompass the process by which the conflicts between them are resolved.

In the "Conjectural Beginning" Kant characterizes culture as "the genuine education of man as man and citizen" (*CB,* 62) and declares its goal to be a "perfect civil constitution" (*CB,* 61n) that would end the conflict between man's two dispositions.[4] At this point Kant evidently considered the development of culture to be part of the history of nature, for what he projected as the natural teleological progress toward the cosmopolitan society in the "Idea for a Universal History" is now discussed as a progression from lower to higher states of culture. The "perpetual peace" associated with a cosmopolitan society would be possible only in the state of "perfect culture" (*CB,* 67).

However, this view of culture as nature's own way of resolving man's conflicts raises questions about its relation to the history of freedom. Indeed it seems to make the history of freedom as the work of man superfluous. The four steps of reason described in the first section of the "Conjectural Beginning" affirmed man's capacity for freedom, but the later parts of the essay that deal with culture have nothing to say about how man has subsequently developed this capacity to actually make himself free. Kant's declaration to his contemporary reader that he must "ascribe his present troublesome conditions to himself and his own choice" (*CB,* 68) assumes a responsibility based on freedom. Yet he also casts doubt on how freely man's past course has been chosen when he says that "the human species is irresistibly turned away from the task assigned to it by nature, the progressive cultivation of its disposition to goodness" (*CB,* 65). Such a statement leaves unclear whether it is nature's secret plan or man's perversity that is irresistible.

Culture as the Ultimate Purpose of Human History

Kant's theories of history set forth in the above popular essays can be brought into the critical framework by means of the reflective approach to teleology of the *Critique of Judgment.* The latter makes it

---

4. For an examination of the relation of Kant's conception of culture to Rousseau's see William A. Galston, *Kant and the Problem of History* (Chicago: University of Chicago Press, 1975), 93–132.

possible for us to reconceive Kant's speculative claims about nature's teleology in the "Idea for a Universal History" as more limited reflective judgments that suspend all realism of purposiveness. Thus instead of being explained as a product of Nature's "intentions" and "secret plans," human history is to be considered as purposive in relation to our reflective theoretical interests. Such purposiveness is neither prescribed to nature nor based on inductive generalizations from experience. It is only by prescribing a principle of purposiveness to ourselves that we can reflect on the telos of nature and history. As previously noted, the teleological judgment has a cognitive dimension (see chapters 3 and 5). Although it does not give determinant explanations, it does more than express our subjective response. Reflective teleological judgments provide descriptions of natural and historical processes in relation to human ends.

The view that man is a natural purpose is brought together with the view that he is a final purpose (*Endzweck*) independent of nature in the idea of the ultimate purpose (*letzter Zweck*) of nature. As noted earlier, the growth of reason establishes man's superiority as a natural purpose relative to other creatures. The idea of man as an ultimate purpose of nature brings in the additional factor that man's destination is to become free from nature and attain moral autonomy as a final purpose. The ultimate purpose of nature regarding man is thus "to prepare him for what he must do himself in order to be a final purpose" (*C3*, §83, 281). With this formulation, the earlier speculative claim about nature's directing the development of man's capacities can be reconciled with the demand of practical reason that only freely chosen actions define man as a moral end in himself. This more balanced perspective in the use of teleological ideas points to a reflective interpretation of history that can be used to counteract the impression given by some of Kant's writings that history and politics can be reduced to a rhetoric of "worldly cleverness"[5] on the one hand and a speculative "dialectic of the passions"[6] on the other hand.

The assertion that man is the ultimate purpose of nature is unusual in suggesting a link between reflective and determinant judgments in historical interpretation. It involves the intersection of a reflective teleological judgment about man as a natural purpose with a determi-

5. Stanley Rosen, *Hermeneutics as Politics* (New York: Oxford University Press, 1987), 45.
6. Rosen, *Hermeneutics*, 47.

nant judgment of practical reason about man as a final purpose. Whereas aesthetic ideas served as felt presentations of rational ideas, the reflective teleological idea of ultimate purpose can be said to contain a historical presentation of the rational idea of a final purpose. With aesthetic ideas, reason guides reflection on the significance or purposiveness of life in general, but this teleological idea guides reflection on what we hold to be true (*fürwahrhalten*) about man's actual purposes.

Kant makes it clear that not all aspects of man's life qualify him to be considered as the ultimate purpose of nature. The latter must be separated from all those purposes made possible through nature alone. According to Kant, this means that we must abstract from happiness or the matter of all man's earthly purposes. Therefore, the ultimate purpose of nature in man is located in only a "formal subjective condition," that is, "the aptitude of setting purposes before himself and (independently of nature in determining his purposes) using nature as a means comfortably to the maxims of his free purposes in general" (*C3*, §83, 281; V, 431). The production of such an aptitude is called "culture (*Cultur*)." Considered as the ultimate purpose of nature, culture enables man to become independent of nature.

Kant had already spoken of the development of culture in the "Conjectural Beginning," but in the *Critique of Judgment* the idea is given greater definition and theoretical clarity. Kant distinguishes two modes of culture: a culture of skill and a culture of discipline.[7] The culture of skill develops man's natural capacities under formal conditions that promote his aptitude for purposes in general. The purposiveness of nature on this score would be fulfilled by ordering man's relations in a "civil society (*Gesellschaft*)" and a "*cosmopolitan whole*" (*C3*, §83, 282; V, 432). Hence the perpetual peace of the cosmopolitan society, which Kant had previously identified with the state of "perfect culture," is now identified with only one of its modes, i.e., the culture of skill. He argues that the culture of skill alone is not sufficient to define man as an ultimate purpose, "for it is not adequate to furthering the *will* in the determination and choice of purposes" (*C3*, §83, 281–82). The cosmopolitan society would provide the optimal historical condition for human culture, but it would not ensure

7. Salim Kemal further distinguishes "culture in general," in which discipline is central, from "moral culture." See *Kant and Fine Art* (Oxford: Clarendon Press, 1986), 225–33.

that man's will is in conformity with the maxims of his free purposes. What is also required for the latter is the culture of discipline, which consists in freeing the will from the "despotism of desires" (*C3*, §83, 282). By this discipline we do not eliminate our natural desires, but gain some rational control over them so that we are no longer tied to sensuous objects alone. The beautiful arts and the sciences contribute to this culture of discipline because they make us "more civilized, if not morally better" and "win us in large measure from the tyranny of sense propensions" (*C3*, §83, 284).

The disciplining of our inclinations is said to be negative, but it points to a positive result in opening us up to purposes that are higher than natural purposes. Kant defines the culture of discipline as a "striving of nature to a cultivation which makes us receptive to higher purposes than nature itself can supply" (*C3*, §83, 283). Although all culture involves a process of nature preparing man to transcend nature, it is the culture of discipline that brings man to the crucial point where he recognizes his aptitude for higher purposes and asserts his independence from purely natural purposes.

Culture in the *Critique of Judgment* is a purpose of nature, but the "nature" of reflective teleology is not viewed as the all-encompassing, providential Nature of the "Idea for a Universal History." Culture then is no longer simply a part of the history of nature, but makes room for a history of freedom. As such the idea of culture can be used to reflect on the way moral purposes are realized in history through the development of our natural capacities and our moral freedom.

Kant also adds a religious dimension to the moral interpretation of history by speaking of the idea of the *highest* purpose in the world. The idea of a highest purpose is the reflective teleological equivalent of the highest good and reintroduces man's hope for happiness, which had been excluded in considering the higher moral purposes of culture.

In the *Critique of Practical Reason* the highest good was described as a synthesis of virtue and happiness, where the attainment of virtue is the condition of being worthy of happiness. Since neither nature nor morality can promise happiness, the highest good is an ideal that is possible only in an intelligible world. The hope for a reconciliation of virtue and happiness, Kant writes, lies in a "Kingdom of God, in which nature and morality come into harmony . . . through a holy Author of the world, who makes possible the desired highest good" (*C2*, 133). In the *Critique of Judgment* the idea of the highest good is related to the reflective teleological system of nature by interpreting it as the highest purpose in this world. Thus instead of placing the highest good in a transcendent Kingdom of God, Kant now speaks of the highest good as "the highest final purpose to be worked out by us" (*C3*, §91, 322). As Yirmiahu Yovel claims, the highest good changes from its earlier status as a "rational version of the notion of the next world" into a this-worldly "historical goal."[8] This does not mean that the highest good becomes a fully secular ideal. The teleological idea of the highest final purpose still points to God to make possible the reconciliation of virtue and happiness. Kant makes this clear in §87 of the *Critique of Judgment* when he claims that the practical necessity of the highest good does not harmonize with its "physical possibility . . . if we connect with our freedom no other causality (as a means) than that of nature. Consequently, we must assume a moral world cause . . . i.e., we must admit that there is a God" (*C3*, §87, 301).

It could seem that relating history to the highest good produces a new form of providential history, which simply replaces speculation about Nature's intention with claims about God's intention. However, Kant is using the idea of God as a moral cause in a mere reflective sense. Whereas the idea of God as a postulate of practical reason is "*constitutive*, i.e., practically determinant" for action, in relation to considerations about the "objective possibility of things" in nature and history it "is a mere *regulative* principle for the reflective judgment" (*C3*, §88, 309).

Because the idea of culture is central to the reflective teleological interpretation of human history, the two modes of culture that define the ultimate purpose of nature can be said to be constitutive of the development of humanity. But since we are not justified in making constitutive cognitive claims on the basis of the reflective teleological idea of culture, Kant also continues to use the moral ideas of God and the highest good as regulative principles for interpreting the highest final purpose in history. Historical interpretation can accordingly be characterized as requiring the intersection of the regulative use of practical reason and the reflective use of teleological judgment. In relation to the natural sciences, the regulative use of ideas of reason held out the hope that the laws of nature are more systematically related

8. Yovel, *Kant and the Philosophy of History* (see chap. 4, n. 16), 72.

than even our finite imagination can suggest. In relation to the interpretation of history, however, the regulative use of ideas of reason serves to counteract any premature imaginative projections of order. By now turning to Kant's discussions of authentic interpretation, it becomes possible to propose that for understanding history the reflective use of teleological ideas must be authenticated by the regulative use of moral ideas.

Religion and Authentic Interpretation

Kant's only extended comments on the problem of interpretation occur in the religious writings that follow the *Critique of Judgment*. The distinction between doctrinal and authentic interpretation that was discussed briefly in chapter 2 above is introduced in the essay "On the Failure of All Attempted Philosophical Theodicies" (1791), where Kant deals with the religious interpretation of nature. The task of a theodicy gives rise to hermeneutical considerations because here the problem is not just one of organizing our theoretical knowledge of nature, but of finding moral meaning and divine wisdom in the telos of nature. As traditionally understood, all theodicy, Kant writes, "must be an interpretation (*Auslegung*) of nature and must show how God manifests the intention (*Absicht*) of his will through it."[9] However, for such a theological reading, nature cannot be considered the open book that it was for the theoretical point of view. According to Kant, nature is especially "a closed book when we want to read the *final* intention (*Endabsicht*) of God (which is always a moral one) from a work which is only an object of experience" (*FPT*, 291; VIII, 264).

Traditional theodicies have given doctrinal rather than authentic interpretations because they have been based on speculations about how nature displays God's intentions.[10] Whereas doctrinal interpretations of the theoretical system of nature were shown to be hypothetical (see chapter 2), doctrinal interpretations of the intentions of God in nature are "sophistical (*vernünftelnd*)" (VIII, 264). Doctrinal theodicies not only seek to systematize the theoretical

9. "On the Failure of All Attempted Philosophical Theodicies" (hereafter *FPT*), trans. Michel Despland, in Despland, *Kant on History and Religion*, 283–97 (Montreal: McGill-Queen's University Press, 1973), 291; VIII, 264.

10. In retrospect, Kant's descriptions of nature's intentions in the "Idea for a Universal History" can be said to be doctrinal.

meaning of experience, but also presume to know what God *meant* nature to accomplish. They read God's intention into the course of human experience so that events seemingly "contrary to purpose (*zweckwidrig*)" (*FPT,* 283; VIII, 255) are interpreted to disclose a deeper divine purpose.

"On the Failure of All Attempted Philosophical Theodicies" was the first essay published after the *Critique of Judgment,* and Kant's criticism of doctrinal interpretation can be understood in light of his newly established theory of reflective judgment. Doctrinal theodicies cannot be justified from the critical standpoint because they make determinant judgments about what is or is not purposive in nature. We have seen that for Kant all claims about purposes in nature are reflective judgments valid only from the human point of view. They cannot show what the object is "*in itself*" or for God, but what it is "*for us* (for men in general)" (*C3,* §90, 314).

Although traditional doctrinal theodicies must by their very nature fail, Kant believes that it is possible to have a more modest but authentic form of theodicy. What Kant calls "an authentic (*authentische*) theodicy" will be based on the same practical reason that leads us to conceive of God as "a moral and wise being" (VIII, 264). Without speculating on how God acts in relation to nature, it affirms the postulate of practical reason that He must somehow relate nature to the highest good for the sake of morality. Such an authentic, moral interpretation does not give a complete explanation of God's plan for nature, but by means of it at least "the letters (*Buchstaben*) of His creation can be given a sense (*einen Sinn*)" (*FPT,* 291; VIII, 264). In the language of the *Critique of Judgment* we can say that an authentic theodicy is an attempt to use our moral idea of God regulatively to guide our reflective judgments about the purposiveness of nature. An authentic interpretation might be called a morally warranted reflective interpretation.

Kant cites the story of Job as an allegorical model of an authentic theodicy. Job's friends give a doctrinal interpretation of his inexplicable suffering by applying the generally accepted teaching that such suffering must represent God's punishment for unknown past sins. Job, however, continues to declare that his suffering is inscrutable to him and refuses their advice to plead for God's forgiveness. While recognizing his share of human frailty and the sovereignty of God's will, he relies on his own conscience, which does not condemn him. According to Kant, Job's rejection of doctrinal explanations is ultimately vindicated by God, who showed him "an ordering of the whole which manifests a wise Creator, although His ways remain inscrutable for us" (*FPT,* 292–93). What matters is "only the uprightness of the heart, not the merit of one's insights, the sincere and undisguised confession of one's doubts, and the shunning of feigned convictions which one does not really feel" (*FPT,* 293; VIII, 266–67).

Thus an authentic theodicy does not seek to explain God's specific intentions in this world, but affirms an overall order reflecting a divine wisdom. Whereas an authentic interpretation of the scientific system of nature is based on experience and the laws of physics, an authentic theodicy is rooted in the laws of morality within us that precede all experience. It appeals to the uprightness of the heart and genuine moral feeling guided by the dictates of conscience. However, in subsequent writings Kant comes to rely less on sincerity of feeling as a mode of authentic interpretation.

The distinction between the authentic and the doctrinal next occurs in the *Religion within the Limits of Reason Alone* (1793), where Kant moves from the interpretation of nature to the interpretation of biblical texts. In this work Kant examines to what extent historical religions founded on revelation can be reconciled with a universal religion based on moral reason. Although no historical faith can make a rightful claim to the universality of rational faith, Kant recognizes that man has a natural need for some common, tangible confirmation of his highest concepts.[11] "The authority of Scripture" is, according to Kant, "at present the only instrument in the most enlightened portion of the world, for the union of all men into one church" (*RWL,* 103). Given this instrumental role of Scripture, its proper interpretation becomes essential.

Kant considers three types of claimants to "the office of interpreter" (*RWL,* 104): (1) those guided by reason, (2) those dependent on scholarship, and (3) those relying on feeling. He dismisses interpretations that are based on "merely an inner *feeling*" (*RWL,* 104) aroused by Scripture. What Kant rejects here are feelings "private to every individual" (*RWL,* 105), rather than aesthetic and moral feelings, which are universal. Kant still calls the moral feeling "unequivocal," but fears

---

11. *Religion within the Limits of Reason Alone* (hereafter *RWL*), trans. T. M. Greene and H. H. Hudson (New York: Harper Torchbooks, 1960), 100.

that it could "lose its dignity through affiliation with fantastical feel-ings of every sort" (*RWL*, 105; VI, 114). Scriptural scholarship evaluat-es the credibility of Scripture and facilitates its interpretation in light of its historical context. Although this kind of historical certification is important, it is subordinate to interpretation by reason. The latter does not aim at a literal interpretation of Scripture nor does it re-produce the intention of its authors. Instead, it proceeds according to "the highest principle of all Scriptural interpretation" (*RWL*, 102; VI, 112): to seek a meaning that will contribute to the moral improvement of all men.

Interpretation using historical scholarship is called "merely *doc-trinal*, having as its end the transformation of ecclesiastical faith for a given people at a given time into a determinate (*bestimmtes*) and en-during system" (*RWL*, 105; VI, 114). Although the aim of doctrinal interpretation is to produce a determinate system that will outlast the revelation of a particular prophet for a specific people, it can never possess more than an empirical generality in that it has historical roots. Only an interpretation based on pure practical reason can be truly universal. Kant calls such an interpretation "*authentic* and valid for the whole world" (*RWL*, 105). In an authentic interpretation the meaning of Scripture will be shown to be in "agreement with the uni-versal practical rules of a religion of pure reason" (*RWL*, 100; VI, 110).

The attributes of doctrinal and authentic interpretations seem to be reversed when Kant subsequently discusses the theologians' in-terpretation of Scripture in relation to church statutes.[12] In the *Conflict of the Faculties* of 1798 he writes: "With regard to what is stat-utory in religion, we may require biblical hermeneutics (*hermeneutica sacra*) . . . to tell us whether the interpreter's findings are to be taken as *authentic* or *doctrinal*. In the first case, interpretation (*Auslegung*) must conform literally (*buchstäblich*) (philologically) with the au-thor's meaning. But in the second case the writer is free, in his interpretation, to ascribe to the text (philosophically) the meaning it admits of for morally practical purposes" (*CF*, 121; VII, 66). Here it is

---

12. The changes discussed here may be due in part to the fact that Kant had been censured by the Prussian authorities for his views in the *Religion within the Limits of Reason Alone*. It is thus possible that some of Kant's claims about biblical hermeneutics and statutory religion are not to be taken at face value. But in any case Kant ends up by reaffirming the superiority of a morally based authentic interpretation of religious texts.

the doctrinal rather than the authentic interpretation that approaches the text more freely in accordance with an a priori moral interest. It is intended to determine "what teaching reason can ascribe (a priori), for the sake of morality, to a biblical text" (*CF*, 123). The authentic interpretation is now associated with a concern for the author's literal meaning. But in addition to this philological authenticity, Kant suggests another kind of authenticity by indicating that the doctrinal interpretation can also be considered authentic. "If a people has been taught to revere a sacred Scripture," Kant writes, "the doctrinal interpretation . . . which looks to the people's moral interest . . . is also the authentic one with regard to its religion: in other words, this is how God wants this people to understand His will as revealed in the Bible" (*CF*, 123). This may be characterized as theologically authentic for a particular religion. The difference between philological and theological authenticity lies in the kinds of intention being interpreted: the former concerns the meaning intended by the human authors of the Scriptures, the latter the will of God himself. The reason why doctrinal interpretation must mediate between them is that "the authors of sacred Scripture, being human, could have made mistakes" (*CF*, 121). The *theological* authenticity that culminates this three-step process of biblical hermeneutics still falls short of an authentic *moral* interpretation as defined in the preceding essays. It aims at understanding God's will rather than the demands of reason.

These changes in the usage of the terms "doctrinal" and "authentic" apply only to the analysis of what is statutory in religion. Since biblical hermeneutics as practiced in the theological faculty aims to expound the statutory content of the Bible, its primary allegiance is to ecclesiastical authority rather than to reason. Statutes, as Kant writes, are "teachings that proceed from an act of choice on the part of an authority (that do not issue directly from reason)" (*CF*, 33). Although the use of doctrinal interpretation by theologians is said to bring a priori rational considerations to bear, its results may be still empirical insofar as its base is statutory and still speculative insofar as theologians use reason dogmatically. Kant ends the discussion of biblical hermeneutics by claiming that the philosopher is always free to subject its results to the critique of reason. Only on the basis of a critical use of moral reason can interpretation be philosophically authentic.

We can thus distinguish three kinds of authenticity in religious interpretation: (1) a philological authenticity that is based on historical scholarship to reconstruct the meaning intended by the human authors of the Bible, (2) theological authenticity that determines God's will on the basis of the authority of a church and its statutes, and finally (3) philosophical or moral authenticity that reflects on the truth of both philological and theological claims on the basis of practical reason.

In the *Religion within the Limits of Reason Alone* we saw Kant acknowledge a natural need to supplement authentic moral interpretation with doctrinal interpretations based on historical texts. This is a need that can be outgrown through an increasing reliance on our own reason. Doctrinal mediation or support will no longer be thought necessary with our recognition that "the God Who speaks through our own (morally practical) reason is an infallible interpreter of His words in the Scriptures, Whom everyone can understand" (*CF*, 123). Yet having the infallible interpreter "within us" (*CF*, 83) only establishes in principle that we can rely on our practical reason for an authentic interpretation. It does not guarantee, of course, that our finite reason will attain true moral insight—particularly in view of Kant's stress on the human propensity to evil in his religious writings. Kant does not treat moral self-knowledge as a problem of interpretation per se, but it is clear that judging the relation between the moral law and our intentions calls for interpretation.

The effort to attain an authentic interpretation of one's moral intentions is complicated by the fact that Kant claims certainty about the moral law on the one hand and uncertainty about our moral response to it on the other hand. In the essay *On the Old Saw: That May Be Right in Theory but It Won't Work in Practice* (1793) Kant claims that moral distinctions "are graven into the human soul in the crudest, most legible script."[13] This means that the moral law is so clearly inscribed in us all that no deciphering is needed to know what our duty is. But it is important to note that only the *letter* of the law can be inscribed in us. Moral worthiness requires us not only to do our duty by following the letter of the law, but also to do so primarily out of respect for the law. This makes it necessary (1) to understand the *spirit* or meaning of the law and (2) to examine our intentions in following the law. Concerning the latter Kant does acknowledge that uncertain-

13. Kant, *On the Old Saw: That May Be Right in Theory but It Won't Work in Practice* (hereafter *TP*), trans. E. B. Ashton (Philadelphia: University of Pennsylvania Press, 1974), 54.

ty will exist: "I gladly admit that no man can ever be conscious with certainty of *having performed* his duty quite unselfishly, for this is a matter of internal experience" (*TP,* 51). Although in his analysis of Job's authentic interpretation, Kant emphasized Job's sincerity and uprightness of heart, he subsequently underscores a "*perversity* of the heart" (*RWL,* 32) that leads us to place self-love ahead of respect for the law. This evil propensity in human nature can give rise to self-deception in the interpretation of our moral intentions.

Given these fundamental ambiguities, the self-certainty manifested in Job's appeal to the dictates of his own conscience is put into question. Conscience, previously appealed to as a support of authentic interpretation, itself becomes subject to interpretation. Instead of simply providing a direct introspective access to our moral intentions, conscience also involves a reference to a judgment by an other. In *The Metaphysical Principles of Virtue* of 1797, Kant writes that "conscience has the peculiarity that though this whole matter is an affair of man with himself, man sees himself, nevertheless, compelled to conduct this affair as though at the bidding of another person."[14] Because the accused and the judge cannot be the same person in the court of conscience, reason projects an ideal other to judge the morality of our intentions. Conscience on these terms is defined as "the subjective principle of being accountable to God for one's deeds" (*MPV,* 102).

In the interpretation of our own moral motives our conscience contains a reference to an ideal, other interpreter. God, as the "'one who knows the heart,'" represents the infallible interpreter, who can "see into the innermost parts of the disposition of each individual" (*RWL,* 91). It would be just as presumptuous, however, to claim to know God's true interpretation of our intentions as it was for doctrinal interpretations to claim to know God's own intentions. Therefore the ideal of a divine determinant judgment can be used only regulatively to guide our own fallible reflective judgments about our moral intentions. To use this ideal constitutively would render morality heteronomous. In the final analysis, it is still our own moral reason that authenticates our reflective interpretations—whether of nature, religious texts, or human agents in history—but it is a reason that must

14. Kant, *Metaphysical Principles of Virtue* (hereafter *MPV*), trans. James Ellington (Indianapolis: Bobbs-Merrill, 1964), 101.

be "enlarged" to include a reference to the other (see chapter 8, on the *sensus communis* as an enlarged mode of thought).

Divinatory History and the Imagination

Kant's views on authentic interpretation can be related to the reflective teleological approach of the *Critique of Judgment* through his discussion of progress in history. In the essay "An Old Question Raised Again: Is the Human Race Constantly Progressing?" [15] Kant distinguishes between three kinds of predictive (*vorhersagende*) history. The first kind, to which Kant does not give a special name, attempts to predict the future on the basis of the known laws of nature. A second kind, which he calls prophetic, or *weissagende,* history, attempts to supplement prediction by making a determinant use of supernatural signs, and is for that reason uncritical. A third kind, called divinatory, or *wahrsagende,* history, also goes beyond the known laws of nature, but does so by using natural rather than supernatural signs. Its claims concerning moral progress in history must be based on some experience in the human race—an actual event that can be considered a "historical sign . . . demonstrating the tendency of the human race viewed in its entirety" (*CF,* 151).

It is clear that the first kind of predictive history aims at a determinant explanation of the future. Were it possible to establish historical laws equivalent to the laws of physics, this kind of history would be authentic in the same sense that the scientific interpretation of nature is authentic (see chapter 2). But the only example Kant gives of this kind of history appeals to eclipses of the sun and moon. This indicates that he does not take it very seriously. Prophetic history using supernatural signs is a religious interpretation of history based on doctrinal speculations. Knowing how critical Kant was of doctrinal interpretations, we can also dismiss this kind of history. The divinatory (*wahrsagende*) history adopted by Kant[16] establishes an intermediate philosophical position between supposed scientific explanations and religious interpretations of history. It can be shown to be both reflec-

15. The essay constitutes the second part of *The Conflict of the Faculties* (*CF*) discussed earlier.

16. Unfortunately, the term "wahrsagende" is not consistently translated. At first it is translated as "divinatory" (see *CF,* 141) but at crucial points in Kant's later discussion it is rendered as "prophetic" (see *CF,* 151, 157).

tive in its use of teleology and authentic in its appeal to a principle in which "there must be something moral" (*CF*, 157). Elsewhere Kant calls *wahrsagen*, or divining the truth, "a natural skill" (*AP*, 61). *Wahrsagende* history thus involves a reflective art of interpreting historical events rather than a determinant science of explaining them.

Kant looks to the French Revolution as an actual event that could be interpreted as a sign of possible historical progress toward the idea of a perfect state, which is defined as having a republican constitution in "Perpetual Peace."[17] But he focuses neither on the causal consequences of the revolution nor on the particular actions or interests of its direct participants. The reason for this is that some of the actual results of the French Revolution did not spell moral progress. For example, in *The Metaphysical Elements of Justice* of 1797 he expressed a moral "horror"[18] at the perversion of justice involved in the formal execution of Louis XVI. Nevertheless, Kant finds a sign of historical progress in the experience of those such as himself who had witnessed the French Revolution from a distance and sympathized with its republican ideals. Just as in the interpretation of a text the author's actual intention is not decisive, the actual intentions of historical agents are not central to *wahrsagende* history, which is concerned with the moral tendency of the human race as a whole. What is significant is the fact that even at a distance the French Revolution aroused in its spectators a "universal yet unselfish participation (*uneigennützige Teilnehmung*) of players on one side against those on the other, even at the risk that their partisanship could become very disadvantageous for them if discovered" (*CF*, 153; VII, 85). The sympathetic response of these spectators makes it possible to interpret the French Revolution as a hopeful sign of progress, for, as Kant writes, their "well-wishing participation . . . can have no other cause than a moral predisposition in the human race" (*CF*, 153; VII, 85).

There has been considerable disagreement about the best way to characterize this response to the French Revolution. To the extent

17. See Kant, "Perpetual Peace," trans. Lewis White Beck, in *Kant on History*, 94. It is in this essay of 1795 that Kant also makes it clear that the idea of Providence as used in the "Idea for a Universal History" cannot be observed or inferred. Any consideration of Providence or design in world history is purely interpretive, because "we can and must supply it from our own minds in order to conceive of its possibility by analogy to actions of human art" ("Perpetual Peace," 107).

18. *The Metaphysical Elements of Justice* (hereafter *MEJ*), trans. John Ladd (Indianapolis: Bobbs-Merrill, 1965), 87n.

that Kant speaks of unselfish spectators, the response seems to be aesthetic.[19] This impression is reinforced by the English translation of *uneigennützige Teilnehmung* as "disinterested sympathy" (a phrase characteristic of the *Critique of Judgment*) rather than as "unselfish participation." Such an aesthetical interpretation fits with Hannah Arendt's conception of the political as the public realm "constituted by the critics and the spectators, not by the actors or the makers."[20] Arendt claims that the spectator is "impartial by definition."[21] This may be true for the disinterested spectator of the aesthetic judgment, but the spectators that Kant refers to here are clearly not impartial. They display a "partisanship" for the republican cause bordering on "enthusiasm," which according to Kant involves a "passionate participation in the Good" (*CF*, 154).[22]

Because the spectator's response to the French Revolution is at the same time aesthetic, teleological, and moral, it is possible to compare it with Kant's account of the sublime. The spectacle of this revolution is marked by a certain "grandeur" (*CF*, 154), and like the sublime it involves a transgression of limits. Both require a shift of perspective to transform what at first glance may be fearsome into something uplifting. Just as our representations of the starry heavens and the ocean are sublime only if we abstract from their actual content, so the French Revolution is sublime only if we abstract from its direct participants and the violence they may have committed. However, there is also an important difference. We saw in chapter 4 that the sublime is terrifying if we judge it purely naturalistically as a phenomenon that overpowers our own physical and empirical capacities. Only by shifting to the moral perspective can we transform the pathological fear of an overwhelming mountain into sublime wonder. But in Kant's response to the French Revolution, it is the legal perspective that produces a sense of moral horror at those direct participants who used the semblance of a "formal execution" (*MEJ*, 88n) to subvert the

19. This is what I emphasized in my book *Dilthey* (see chap. 3, n. 5), 19–20, in order to explore the idea of an aesthetic of history in Kant and Dilthey.

20. Hannah Arendt, *Kant's Political Philosophy* (see intro., n. 1), 63.

21. Arendt, *Kant's Political Philosophy*, 55.

22. Similarly we need not assume with Ronald Beiner that the model subject of reflective judgment is a disinterested aesthetic spectator who must be sharply distinguished from the active participant qua subject of the prudential judgment of Aristotelian *phronesis*. (See Ronald Beiner, *Political Judgment* [Chicago: University of Chicago Press, 1983], 102–109).

basis of political institutions. By then going back to the response of the indirect participants it becomes possible to replace a moral condemnation of revolution with reflection about the teleological and moral incentives that inspire revolutionary enthusiasm.

Whatever value the comparison of Kant's account of the sublime and his response to the French Revolution may have, it is crucial to understand the latter as part of an attempt to delineate a mode of *wahrsagende* history in which reflective teleological and determinant practical judgments intersect. Only in this way can interpretation relate the contingency of historical fact to the search for the essential meaning and purposiveness of human life. *Wahrsagende* history uses a particular historical event as a sign that not only intimates a better future for the human race, but also confirms a moral predisposition that can help to bring it about. We can see here the movement of reflective judgment from particular to universal with the French Revolution serving as a historical intimation of the universal confederation of republican states projected by the teleological idea of a cosmopolitan society. Such a reflective interpretation is authenticated by a universal moral tendency disclosed in the historical experience of the spectator-participant.

To claim historical progress on the basis of an enthusiastic moral response seems to bring us back to the authentic theodicy exemplified by Job's uprightness of heart. However, the response of the spectator-participants involves no judgment about their own moral intentions or conscience, and indicates a more general "mode of thinking (*Denkungsart*)" (*CF*, 153; VIII, 85) that shows the moral character and destiny of the human race at large. As in the case of the judgment of taste, we have here a reflective mode of judgment that aims at a social consensus and appeals to a *sensus communis* (see chapter 8). For Kant practical reason must ultimately authenticate the interpretation of history, but no simple determinant judgment based on reason alone can grasp the historical meaning of particular events. For the "authentic" interpretation of historical progress it is necessary to reformulate determinant claims of practical reason in terms of the reflective framework defined by such teleological ideas as culture and a cosmopolitan society. This involves a process of cultural and social mediation to which the imagination contributes more than we have indicated so far.

One reason that the imagination may not appear to make a substantial contribution to an authentic moral interpretation of history is that Kant generally relates the imagination to the interests of our natural desires. The imagination's activities are thus associated with concerns for earthly happiness that distract from the demands of duty. This moral distrust of the imagination was reflected in Kant's criticism of those who react to present suffering by looking back to an imagined paradise instead of striving for a future moral improvement.

Nonetheless, we also saw in the "Conjectural Beginning" that the imagination aided the early development of reason in going beyond the bounds of instinctual knowledge. Although the imagination can lead to abuses of reason by introducing artificial desires, its contribution is necessary to achieve a better use of reason. Kant spoke too of the imagination as rendering our inclinations more inward and ideal. This more positive view of the imagination's activity can be developed in relation to the theory of culture in the third *Critique* because the purposes of culture were specifically defined as excluding any interest in earthly happiness. The imagination in aesthetic judgment can contribute to the growth of culture because it involves a disinterested aesthetic pleasure. Indeed, we can say that judgments of taste concerning beauty enhance the culture of discipline, for they replace the charms of sense with a disinterested pleasure in a representation of the imagination. This gives added significance to Kant's claim in the Critique of Aesthetic Judgment that "taste makes possible the transition, without any violent leap, from the charm of sense to habitual moral interest" (*C3*, §59, 200).

In terms of its basic function of mediating between sense and reason, the role of the imagination was evident in producing the normal and aesthetic ideas that function as rules for reflective interpretation. This is not so apparent in teleological interpretations. Teleological ideas are not always products of the imagination insofar as they are often viewed as concepts based on descriptions of natural purposes. Nor is the imagination generally involved in setting a final moral purpose, since according to Kant the moral law is directly accessible as a "fact of reason" (see chapter 6). In the *Critique of Practical Reason* he maintains that the imagination is not even needed to schematize the moral law in order to apply it to particular circumstances. Whereas concepts of the understanding require *schemata* of the transcendental imagination in order to be applicable to objects of experience, an idea of practical reason needs only a natural law of the understanding as the *type* that exhibits the moral law (see *C2*, 71). The isomorphism between laws of morality and laws of nature highlighted by the typic of pure practical judgment is simply that no exceptions can be allowed. To understand this formal relation between the laws of morality and nature requires no mediation by the imagination.

However, the imagination does play a mediating role in the historical presentation of teleological ideas that relate natural and moral purposes. The reconciliation of happiness and virtue in the highest good is presented by the imagination as the highest purpose in history. In projecting this historical goal or ideal, the imagination can make use of religious imagery, which Kant speaks of as schematic and symbolic. A historical religion, he writes, can serve as a "visible representation (the schema) of an invisible kingdom of God on earth" (*RWL*, 122). Similarly, Kant states that the biblical account of the end of the world "may be interpreted as a symbolical representation" (*RWL*, 125) of a rational end. While the moral law may not need its mediation, the imagination helps to approximate the ideal of the highest purpose in history by means of a "schema" or symbolic representation of an ethical commonwealth. Thus the teleological idea of a cosmopolitan society specifies and gives imaginative content to the abstract ideal of an invisible kingdom of God on earth.

Finally, the imagination is involved in the use of a historical experience as a sign of progress in history. A historical sign is more concrete and empirical than any aesthetic or religious symbol, but it still requires the imagination. In the *Anthropology* the power of using signs is regarded as an extension of the imagination and defined as "the ability to recognize the present as the means for connecting representations of foreseen events with those of past events" (*AP*, 64; VII, 191). In Kant's interpretation of the French Revolution as an example of divinatory history, a present response to an actual past event becomes the basis of foreseeing the future as leading to a republican state and a cosmopolitan society. The imagination is obviously important in such an interpretation, since any past event or future goal is by nature not directly intuitable. A divinatory history that anticipates progress toward a reflectively conceived telos must rely on the imagination to recognize the sign of a universal moral tendency in a particular factual event. The imagination here serves reason in the authentic moral interpretation of history. It allows divinatory (*wahrsagende*) history to be truth-telling (*wahr-sagend*) and to specify a moral truth.

8
Common Sense and Transcendental Orientation in Hermeneutics

Having opened up the hermeneutical implications of the third *Critique,* I will consider the more general relation between transcendental philosophy and hermeneutics in this final chapter. From the contemporary hermeneutical standpoint the main shortcoming of Kant's transcendental philosophy is that it is foundational and appeals to a priori starting points that are not subject to reevaluation. However, the previous chapters have shown that the *Critique of Judgment* does not simply rely on the fixed rules and archetypes of the first *Critique.* The principle of reflective judgment is adaptive to the particular contents of experience and articulates order through the mutual adjustment of parts and wholes. Normal, aesthetic, and teleological ideas present types or models that provide indeterminate and revisable guidelines for interpretation.

The appeal to transcendental conditions can also be reconceived in relation to the problem of interpretation. Referring back to the transcendental conditions of the subject means one thing for systematizing physics (see chapter 2) and something else for the interpretation involved in dealing with the aesthetic, religious, and cultural dimensions of human life (see chapters 6 and 7). In the former, interpretation is primarily theoretical and can be derived from the transcendental conditions of the determinant judgment. In the latter, interpretation is evaluative and must be derived from the transcendental conditions of reflective judgment. It will be argued in this chapter that the transcendental conditions of determinant judgment are foundational, but that those of reflective judgment are what I would call "orientational." The importance of orientation for reflective interpretation can be seen in both the idea of common sense and the feeling of life that are central to the third *Critique.*

Imaginative Orientation and Critical Interpretation

In his essay "What Is Orientation in Thinking?" (1786), Kant describes orientation in its most basic sense as a process whereby I proceed from one quadrant of my field of vision to the other three which make up my horizon. I relate what I see in front of me to the other quadrants by means of a "feeling of a distinction concerning my own subject, namely, that of my right and left hand."[1] The distinction between right and left, which is an immediate sensory discrimination based on a bodily feeling, is indispensable in relating the quadrants of my spatial field into a coherent perspective on objective nature. Here the imagination relates what is directly given to me to what is only indirectly present within my horizon by means of a feeling that is subjective, but not in any private sense, for it is already aimed at a public environment. This nature-orienting function of the imagination could be said to be presupposed by all its other functions. Indeed, looking back to the synoptic image formation (*Abbildung*) that was central in Kant's precritical writings (see chapter 1), we can now say that such a use of the imagination provides an indispensable orientational background for the experiential syntheses of the imagination in the *Critique of Pure Reason*.

After having defined imaginative orientation spatially in relation to nature, Kant then applies the idea of orientation to thought that transcends the bounds of our experience of nature. To orient myself in thought is to allow myself to be guided by a subjective principle of reason when objective principles are not obtainable. In this manner Kant traces the rational idea of God back to a subjectively felt need of reason (see *WOT,* 298; VIII, 139). He shows that Moses Mendelssohn's appeal to the idea of God on the basis of a so-called sound or common reason (see *WOT,* 299–300; VIII, 140) is really an appeal to a subjective belief of reason.

Kant's essay "What Is Orientation in Thinking?" distinguishes two kinds of orientation: the spatial orientation of the perceiving self to a natural environment and the mental orientation of the thinking self to

---

1. "What Is Orientation in Thinking?" (hereafter *WOT*), trans. L. W. Beck, in *Kant's "Critique of Practical Reason" and Other Writings on Moral Philosophy,* ed. L. W. Beck (Chicago: University of Chicago Press, 1949), 295; VIII, 134.

the transcendent realm. In the *Critique of Judgment* Kant speaks briefly of judgment orienting itself, which suggests the possibility of a
more reflective model of orientation. He points out that the reflective
principle of purposiveness provides us "with concepts amid the immense variety of nature (so that judgment can orient itself [*orientiren
zu können*])" (*C3*, intro., viii, 30; V, 193; see Pluhar, 33). The concepts
of purposiveness used to orient reflective judgment concerning
nature's immense variety can be either aesthetic or teleological. On
the level of judgment it is then possible to propose two reflective
counterparts to orientation in space and thought: namely, an aesthetic orientation that evaluates the world on the basis of the feeling of
life and a teleological orientation that interprets culture on the basis
of common sense or the *sensus communis*.

   In chapter 5 it was claimed that the feeling of life is a responsiveness
to the world that constitutes a transcendental condition of both the
active power of the understanding and the passive power of sense.
The positive pleasure found in beauty was defined as the feeling of the
enhancement of our life; the negative pleasure found in the sublime
was described as the feeling of both a restriction and release of the
vital powers. These feelings of life orient us as we judge the things
around us as either adding to or detracting from the value of our existence. They help us to evaluate the significance of things in relation to
life as a whole just as our spatial feeling relates us to nature as a whole.
The mental feeling of the enhancement of life in aesthetic pleasure
and that of its diminution in displeasure involve immediate discriminations analogous to the direct bodily feeling of the distinction
between left and right that orients us in space. Aesthetic discrimination relates to reflective judgments about the world as the spatial
feeling of right and left relates to determinant judgments about
nature. Both are subjective, but constant, feelings that provide the
necessary orientation as the imagination moves from what is directly
given to what is only indirectly given.

   While aesthetic orientation rooted in the feeling of life can be seen
as the reflective counterpart of our sense of spatial orientation, the
teleological orientation that applies common sense to culture can be
regarded as the reflective counterpart of orientation in thought.
Common sense can orient the judgment of the individual to the larger

perspective of the community and thus provides the basis for what Kant calls an enlarged mode of thought or interpretation.

As first discussed in the Critique of Aesthetic Judgment the idea of common sense is a presupposition for the universal communicability of feeling. Because of its identification with aesthetic feeling, the broader implications of Kant's theory of common sense (including its teleological application to culture) have not been adequately recognized. According to Hans-Georg Gadamer, Kant's transcendental theory of common sense represents an unfortunate dissipation of the humanist common-sense tradition. This tradition, going back to Cicero, Vico, and Shaftesbury, regards common sense as a mode of knowledge rooted in the moral and civic community. It is this sense of tradition as a mode of knowing that Gadamer reappropriates as the framework of his philosophical hermeneutics.[2] In his view, Kant's common sense is an aesthetic, noncognitive alternative to traditional common sense that has led nineteenth-century hermeneutics into a subjective cul-de-sac.[3] However, it is precisely through common sense that the aesthetic judgment can be intersubjective as well as subjective. According to Kant, common sense makes it possible to represent the "subjective necessity" of the judgment of taste as "objective" (*C3*, §22, 76) in the sense of claiming universal assent. More importantly, however, Kant goes on to make the broader claim that common sense is a presupposition of the communicability of *knowledge*. He asserts that "common sense is assumed . . . as the necessary condition of the universal communicability of our knowledge, which is presupposed in every logic and in every principle of knowledge that is not sceptical" (*C3*, §21, 76). This cognitive dimension of Kant's theory of common sense means that it cannot be simply restricted to agreement about taste, as Gadamer assumes, but applies to reflective judgment in general.

Kant himself broaches these more general implications in §40 of the *Critique of Judgment* when he distinguishes between (1) common

2. Hans-Georg Gadamer, *Wahrheit und Methode,* 2d ed. (Tübingen: J. C. B. Mohr, 1965), 28–39.

3. For a more detailed response to these charges than is possible here, see Rudolf Makkreel, "Tradition and Orientation in Hermeneutics," *Research in Phenomenology* 16 (1986): 73–85.

sense as the common or vulgar understanding of men and (2) the common sense as *sensus communis,* or a communal sense (*gemeinschaftlicher Sinn*), that accounts for universal agreement (see *C3,* §40, 136; V, 293). It is important to note that Kant's analysis deals primarily with the *sensus communis* in a generic sense. When relating common sense to judgments of taste, Kant specifies it as aesthetic common sense (*sensus communis aestheticus*). In this context he designates common understanding as logical common sense (*sensus communis logicus*) (see *C3,* §40, 138).

The *sensus communis* uses reflective judgment to abstract from the private empirical aspects of our subjective representations in order to generate what might be called a communal or intersubjective perspective. Whereas vulgar or common understanding designates those beliefs that are actually found to be held in common, the *sensus communis* is an a priori sense that relates us to all of humanity. The *sensus communis* is defined as

> the idea of a sense *common to all,* i.e., of a faculty of judgment which, in its reflection, takes account (a priori) of the mode of representation of all other men in thought, in order, as it were, to compare its judgment with the collective reason of humanity, and thus to escape the illusion arising from the private conditions that could be so easily taken for objective. (*C3,* §40, 136; V, 293)

Instead of being divorced from the common sense that is embodied in Gadamer's concept of the hermeneutic tradition, Kant's *sensus communis* may be understood as articulating the transcendental conditions of traditional common sense. As part of a critical hermeneutics, a theory of common sense seeks the conceptual clarification of the conditions for not only the appeal *to* tradition, but also the equally necessary appeal *from* tradition neglected in the Gadamerian theory. The *sensus communis* provides a mode of orientation to the tradition that allows us to ascertain its relevance to ultimate questions of truth. It is transcendental, not in the sense of providing building blocks for truth, but in the sense of opening up the reflective horizon of communal meaning in terms of which the truth can be determined.

Orientation allows us to relate our own standpoint to a larger perspective that is indirectly given. The relation between the directly and indirectly given—conceived generally by Kant in terms of the imagination and spatial or aesthetic discrimination—is also central to any theory of interpretation guided by common sense. It involves the part-whole relation of the object to its horizon, and of the text to its context, as formulated by the hermeneutic circle. But if we define the relation between our experience and its context as a simple part-whole relation, all interpretation becomes relative to our particular context or tradition. By applying Kant's spatial metaphor of orientation to the hermeneutic circle, we can transform a dyadic relation of part to whole into a triadic one which includes the subject. My spatial horizon must have not only the focal point of some object before me, but also my feeling of orientation toward it as focused in my subject. By means of the relation of these two reference points to each other and to the horizon, I can gain a kind of reflective leverage on the world, which is precisely what is needed in hermeneutics as well.

Current writings which claim that all experience is theory-laden and context-dependent have placed a one-sided emphasis on the fact that every object is oriented *by* its horizon. But it is also important to recognize that the subject orients itself *to* both object and horizon. We can distinguish between ordinary judgments of experience, which are oriented *by* our theoretical framework, and immediate discriminatory judgments, which orient us *to* our theoretical framework. A discriminatory judgment is thus not isolated from our experience at large, but it is not wholly dependent on experience. If orientation is derived only from our horizon, then interpretation is liable to become historicized or tradition-bound. The tradition and its authority would become overwhelming if we could not touch base with those transcendental conditions of our sensibility and common humanity that make critical reflection possible.

Kant himself explicates the critical role of the *sensus communis* in relation to three maxims of the common human understanding: "(1) to think for oneself; (2) to put ourselves in thought in the place of everyone else; (3) always to think consistently" (C3, §40, 136). The first maxim is the maxim of understanding or unprejudiced thought, and the third is the maxim of reason. The second, which Kant calls the maxim of "enlarged thought (*erweiterten Denkungsart*)" (C3, §40, 136; V, 294), is the maxim of judgment; it is the one most relevant to what was quoted earlier about the communal sense comparing its judgment with "the collective reason of humanity."

The maxim of enlarged thought elucidates Kant's assertion that the *sensus communis* involves "comparing our judgment with the possible rather than the actual judgment of others" (*C3*, §40, 136). This comparison with what is possible rather than actual indicates that the imagination has an important role to play in enlarging our thought. Enlargement does not call for us to transpose ourselves into the actual standpoint of someone else. The understanding of the other is dependent on a prior enlargement of one's own thought based on imagining possibilities that are not merely variations of the self. This is not to be confused with the Romantic idea of empathy. Instead of projecting ourselves into the other, we are to project a possible intermediary position held neither by the self nor by the other. This provides a perspective, based on the *sensus communis,* that makes possible a better understanding of both the self and the other.

The hermeneutic ideal of understanding an author better than he understood himself may similarly be conceived as an instance of enlarged thought, which also draws on common sense. This ideal is usually associated with the hermeneutics of Schleiermacher and Dilthey, but it was already formulated by Kant in his discussion of Plato's ideas in the *Critique of Pure Reason*.[4] There Kant shows his usage of the term "idea" to be a critical appropriation of the traditional meaning related to Plato's theory, and he writes:

> I shall not engage here in any literary enquiry into the meaning which this illustrious philosopher attached to the expression. I need only remark that it is by no means unusual, upon comparing the thoughts which an author has expressed in regard to his subject, whether in ordinary conversation or in writing, to find that *we understand him better than he has understood himself.* As he has not sufficiently determined his concept, he has sometimes spoken, or even thought, in opposition to his own intention. (*C1*, A313–14/B370, emphasis added)

4. Martin Redeker reports that Herder spoke of understanding an author better than he understood himself in a letter concerning the study of theology which is dated the same year as the *Critique of Pure Reason*. This could indicate a more general origin. See Redeker's introduction to Dilthey, *Gesammelte Schriften,* vol. 14 (Göttingen: Vandenhoeck & Ruprecht, 1966), liv.

To determine the "literary" details of Plato's meaning is no more Kant's goal than was scholarly exegesis of the author's intentions in the hermeneutics of the *Religion within the Limits of Reason Alone*. Discerning the author's fundamental intention should not be decisive, because some of what is said by the author may be in conflict with it. Kant seeks neither to reproduce Plato's meaning of "idea" nor to legislate his own meaning. Indeed, he declares that those who have the interests of philosophy at heart must "be careful to preserve the expression 'idea' in its original meaning" (*C1*, A319/B376). In light of the *sensus communis,* this original meaning may be said to represent the true or communal meaning available to enlarged thought. Plato's contribution to this meaning lies in his recognition that reason naturally transcends the bounds of experience and that its ideas "are by no means mere fictions of the brain" (*C1*, A314/B371) even though they have no experiential objects that coincide with them. Kant emphasizes the value of Plato's approach for the practical use of reason. However, with regard to Plato's theoretical use of ideas, we should not "follow him . . . in the extravagances whereby he, so to speak, hypostatised them." Kant concedes that Plato's "exalted language" does admit of "milder interpretation appropriate (*angemessenen*) to the nature of things" (*C1*, A314n/B371n; III, 247n).

Ultimately, Kant's claim to understand Plato's theory of ideas better than Plato himself is indicative of his Enlightenment faith in conceptual clarification.[5] We have seen, however, that Kant is not aiming at a literal reconstruction of an author's viewpoint, but at an interpretation based on the principle of the *sensus communis* just discussed. The

---

5. The goal of understanding an author better than he understood himself, shared by Kant, Schleiermacher, and Dilthey, is criticized by Gadamer for reflecting the Enlightenment background of traditional hermeneutics. According to Gadamer, it betrays an unwarranted faith in method and aims at an impossible reconstruction, which must be opposed by the realization that to understand is always to "understand differently" (*Wahrheit und Methode,* 280). It should be pointed out, however, that Schleiermacher and Dilthey conceived the claim for better understanding differently than Kant. Schleiermacher's claim was not based on an Enlightenment faith in conceptual clarification, but on the Romantic assumption that the work of an author stems from an unconscious seminal decision or unifying core, which the reader must attempt to recreate. Dilthey recognizes that such a seminal decision is an explanative schema that conflicts with historical understanding and that its recreation is impossible. For Dilthey better understanding requires us to relate a work to its socio-cultural context. This mode of better understanding already forces us to "understand differently."

ideal of better understanding is primarily a function of reflective judgment and the maxim of enlarged thought that attempts to mediate the actual viewpoints of the other and the self. But the maxims of understanding and reason, which are more directly associated with the Enlightenment, also play a role.

Whereas the maxim of judgment based on common sense encourages us to overcome illusions arising from the private conditions of the self, the maxim of the understanding (*Verstand*)—to think for oneself—encourages us to overcome prejudices inherited from the tradition. From Gadamer's point of view, the common sense of tradition must preserve certain prejudices as unavoidable conditions for human understanding (*Verstehen*). For him the Enlightenment demand that we overcome all prejudice is itself a prejudice.[6] But it is interesting to note that Kant himself gives a more qualified definition of the goal of enlightenment, namely, as "deliverance from superstition" (*C3*, §40, 137), where superstition is considered a *gross* prejudice. This definition suggests that Kant does not expect to eradicate all prejudices or all forms of authority. Just as we know from the *Critique of Pure Reason* that not all illusions can be overcome—that some metaphysical illusions are ineradicable—so we can never be sure that all prejudices can be overcome.

By looking at the interplay of Kant's maxims, we can suggest a complex response to tradition. To think for oneself serves the Enlightenment goal of "man's release from his self-incurred tutelage."[7] But it could have the narrowing effect of simply rejecting one's tradition and lapsing into presentism. This is counterbalanced by the maxim of enlarged thought by which we determine what we have in common with the tradition. Finally, the maxim of reason or consecutive thought serves to test our inherited beliefs for their consistency.

What results is a critical confrontation with tradition whereby we recognize what is a mere prejudice and not a basis for universal understanding. This recognition is made possible by the *sensus communis*. Having distinguished between the *sensus communis* and common or vulgar understanding, Kant provides a basis for discriminating between what is essentially communal in our tradition and what has survived simply on the basis of authority. As was suggested earlier,

6. Gadamer, *Wahrheit und Methode*, 255.
7. Kant, "What Is Enlightenment?" *Kant on History* (see chap. 7, n. 3), 3.

the *sensus communis* is a mode of orientation that must be found in each of us. Given its transcendental status, the *sensus communis* allows us to either assent to or dissent from what is commonly held.

Common Sense and Kant's Transcendental Topology

We have seen that common sense is not merely tied to the aesthetic problems of the *Critique of Judgment,* and have indicated that it is a theoretical presupposition for the communicability of all knowledge. For Kant to link his critical epistemology to common sense may seem surprising, since the Copernican revolution of the *Critique of Pure Reason* is usually interpreted as doing violence to common sense. To be sure, the suppositions that "objects must conform to our knowledge" (*C1,* B xvi) and that our understanding legislates the fundamental structures of nature go against the realism of common sense. Similarly, Kant's argument that the world cannot be given as a measurable whole, either finite or infinite, defies the expectations of common sense. However, the traditional common sense that is violated in the first *Critique* is what Kant calls common human understanding, not the *sensus communis* or communal sense of the third *Critique.*

Turning from the theoretical to the practical sphere, we see that there is no ultimate conflict between the critical perspective and the common human understanding. In the *Foundation of the Metaphysics of Morals,* Kant declares that "the most remarkable thing about the common understanding (*gemeine Verstand*) in its practical concern is that it may have as much hope as any philosopher of hitting the mark."[8] And in the *Critique of Practical Reason,* Kant goes so far as to claim that the "justification of moral principles as principles of a pure reason could be made with sufficient certainty through merely appealing to the judgment of common human understanding (*gemeinen Menschenverstandes*)" (*C2,* 95; V, 91). The expression is often misleadingly translated as "common sense" rather than "common human understanding," but any kind of moral *sense* is inappropriate from the perspective of pure practical reason. What common human under-

---

8. Kant, *Foundation of the Metaphysics of Morals,* trans. Lewis White Beck (Indianapolis: Bobbs-Merrill, 1959), 21; IV, 404.

standing—Kant also speaks here of "common reason"—must do is to make sure that nothing empirical is allowed as a determining condition of a moral principle.

In the third *Critique* Kant is less concerned with the common human understanding of the first two *Critiques* and uncovers a *sensus communis* (a sense that is common to all) that is a transcendental condition of his critical epistemology. The *sensus communis* is necessary for the communication of feeling without concepts. This is a presupposition that applies not only to aesthetic feeling in the judgment of taste, but also to the felt harmonies among the faculties in cognition. We saw in chapter 3 that "*all* cognition" requires an *accord* of the faculties and that the systematic concerns of "cognition *in general*" require an *agreement* of the faculties. These formal relations of accord and agreement among the cognitive faculties are discerned through feeling and communicated through a *sensus communis*. It should be noted that while the agreement of the faculties necessary for cognition *in general* produces aesthetic pleasure, the felt accord necessary for *all* cognition is not an aesthetic feeling.

Kant describes common sense as an "indeterminate norm . . . actually presupposed by us" (*C3,* §22, 77), but leaves its exact epistemological status unclear. He does not explicitly answer his own question: "Whether there is in fact such a common sense, as a constitutive principle of the possibility of experience, or whether a yet higher principle of reason makes it only into a regulative principle for producing in us a common sense for higher purposes" (*C3,* §22, 77).[9]

Since the *sensus communis* is never shown to ground knowledge or to aim at a higher purpose of reason, it is neither constitutive nor regulative in relation to determinant judgments of experience. As a condition of reflective judgment, common sense can be constitutive for aesthetic feeling and regulative for specific teleological claims about nature. But relative to the general problem of the communication of scientific knowledge the transcendental role of the *sensus communis* may be seen to exhibit another aspect, namely, what I have called its orientational function.

9. Manfred Kuehn assumes that Kant adopts the latter alternative of common sense as a regulative principle because "common sense as taste is intimately connected with practical reason and can ultimately be understood only in relation to it." See Manfred Kuehn, *Scottish Common Sense in Germany, 1768–1800* (Kingston: McGill-Queen's University Press, 1987), 201.

The conception of a transcendental *sensus communis* helps to draw out a relation between reflection and orientation that can now be related to Kant's topological language at the end of the Analytic of the *Critique of Pure Reason*. In the appendix "The Amphiboly of Concepts of Reflection" Kant describes "reflection (*Überlegung [reflexio]*)" (*C1*, A260/B316; III, 214) as a process of considering representations in relation to the cognitive faculty to which they belong rather than according to their relation to objects. In judging whether representations belong to the pure understanding or to sensible intuition, *transcendental reflection* compares them in terms of four sets of relations that they can have to each other in the mind: identity and difference, agreement and opposition, inner and outer, matter and form. These four pairs of comparative concepts are called "concepts of reflection." They allow us to discriminate the subjective conditions of experience—unlike concepts of the understanding, which refer to objects of experience.

Transcendental reflection uses these comparative subjective concepts to orient us before we make objective claims about the world. That is, it assigns the *"transcendental location"* (*C1*, A268/B324) of representations either in sensibility or in pure understanding. Thus Kant writes, "The decision as to the place which belongs to every concept according to difference in the use to which it is put, and the direction for determining this place for all concepts according to rules, is a *transcendental topic*" (*C1*, A268/B324). It is through this transcendental topic that Kant attacks Leibniz's intellectual system for its failure to recognize sensibility as a separate source of knowledge so that certain intuitive differences of the phenomenal world remain indiscernible (see *C1*, A270/B326). A transcendental topic or topology, we may say, provides the initial orientation to our judgment as it interprets reality in terms of the phenomenal and noumenal.

The traditional topics of Aristotle and Vico use common sense to survey the contents of reality generically before any definite understanding is possible. In his discussion of a transcendental topic, Kant makes only a passing reference to Aristotle's topics of logical commonplaces, and therefore does not remind us of the role of common sense in traditional topics. Properly, Kant's transcendental topics should be related to a transcendental *sensus communis*. By considering the transcendental reflection of the first *Critique* in light of reflective judgment and the *sensus communis* of the third *Critique* we can expand the notion of a transcendental topic to include not only the formal discrimination of the cognitive faculties as irreducible sources of knowledge, but also their felt accord and agreement, which must be communicated to produce a scientific consensus. The universality of judgments of transcendental reflection presupposes that its comparative "concepts of reflection" (such as agreement and opposition, inner and outer) are really formal discriminations of the *sensus communis*.

We can now summarize the place of common sense in the critical system. Kant's Copernican revolution calls into question some of the *content* of the common understanding, but not the *formal* discriminations implicit in the *sensus communis*. The formal distinctions of a transcendental topology can withstand the critique of pure reason if they are not taken as determinate claims of the understanding, but merely as providing a kind of preunderstanding that orients the subject to the world. The link between transcendental reflection and reflective judgment makes it possible to underscore the nonsynthetic character of reflection in Kant. The function of reflection is generally orientational and can be seen as a transcendental analogue to the imagination's initial task of synoptic image formation. Reflection (*Überlegung*) provides the necessary background for a critical interpretation (*Auslegung*) of nature and history.

Reflective Interpretation and the Human Sciences

The transcendental orientation provided by the feeling of life and the *sensus communis*, together with the use of aesthetic and teleological ideas, supplies an interpretive context encompassing the system of nature as well as human history and culture. The third *Critique* thus establishes a reflective framework within which the relationship between the natural and human sciences can be clarified.

Although Kant did not distinguish the human sciences from the natural sciences, the conception of interpretation that has been developed from his theories of imagination and reflective judgment involves the hermeneutic understanding characteristic of the human sciences. The synthetic imagination of the first *Critique* served the interests of the natural sciences in the systematic interpretation and the objective meaning of our experience of nature (see chapter 2). By contrast, the reflective, nonsynthetic functions of the imagination that are found in the *Critique of Judgment* contribute to reflective interpretation and the broader search in the human sciences for the significance and purposiveness of life (see chapter 3). Here attention is shifted from an abstract worldless ego to a human subject responding to the world. Whereas logical transcendental conditions are valid for any finite intellect, the reflective sense of the transcendental also locates specifically human conditions of consciousness.

Kant's rationalistic heritage led him to assume that the theoretical horizon of our understanding must be fixed in terms of rational ideas and a system of nature modeled on the physical sciences. This perspective is expanded in the third *Critique* to include the biological sciences and the indeterminate ideas of the imagination, but Kant's discussions of culture and history are still conceived within the system of nature framed by rational ideas. Kant's framework can no longer be accepted as adequate for interpreting human life, for as Dilthey and Husserl have shown, the system of nature is abstracted from an original life-nexus or life-world. It is in this less determinate framework of the life-world that interpreting subjects must ultimately find their bearings. Reflection on the life-world provides the preunderstanding or background for both the natural and the human sciences. This background has been widely recognized for interpretation in the human sciences, which deal with the common beliefs and traditions, the cultural and historical factors that comprise our life experience, but its relation to the scientific explanation of nature has yet to be fully analyzed. The natural sciences may abstract from the life-world in explaining the processes of nature, but our discussions linking transcendental reflection and reflective judgment have helped to show how scientific knowledge presupposes a prior orientation to the world. Thus despite the limitations of Kant's framework, the development of his views on the *sensus communis* and the feeling of life serves to conceptualize certain aspects of our preunderstanding of the life-world as modes of transcendental orientation.

Of course it will be important to keep in mind that Kant does not draw the same conclusions as contemporary theorists of the human sciences. For example, the existence of preunderstanding is often used to argue that the human sciences have a special access to the life-world. For Vico and Dilthey the human sciences have an advantage over the natural sciences because they investigate what man himself has made. The *verum-factum* thesis seems to be intimated by Kant when he claims in the *Reflexionen* that "we comprehend only what we can make ourselves" (*RL*, 2398; XVI, 345; 1769–72). In the *Critique of Pure Reason* he also writes "Reason has insight only into that which it produces after a plan of its own" (*C1*, B xiii). But these assertions pertain solely to theoretical reason and its access to nature. Kant construes making or producing in formal terms so that it applies to the mathematical and categorial structures that the human mind extends to nature. The formal structures that we legislate do not render nature directly transparent; they merely constrain it "to give answers to questions of reason's own determining" (*C1*, B xiii). These are questions that admit of "*confirmation or refutation by experiment*" (*C1*, B xix, n). Kant does not think that we can know cultural history, which is manmade, better than nature. Because our own inner experience and the historical consequences of our actions are not readily subjected to experimentation and mathematical measurement, they are considered to be less accessible to theoretical reason than are natural processes.

Kant does provide our practical reason with access to our moral nature insofar as it engraves the moral law into our souls. However, this does not mean that we are fully transparent to ourselves as moral beings. As we saw in chapter 7, our conscience is not always subject to direct rational introspection. Moral self-understanding also requires interpretation using reflective judgments about our moral intentions. The need to supplement the determinant principles of reason with the reflective principle of judgment is especially important if human history is to be interpreted from a moral perspective. Yet the neo-Kantians of the Baden School who have attempted to apply Kant's moral philosophy to the understanding of history have overlooked the significance of reflective judgment. Wilhelm Windelband and Heinrich Rickert developed a theory of the cultural sciences (*Kultur-wissenschaften*) primarily on the basis of the *Critique of Practical Reason*. Ideas of reason are combined with other concepts to form complexes defined as values. These values can guide historical and cultural inquiry much in the way that Weberian ideal types function in the social sciences. Values and ideal types can be likened to the regulative rational ideas of the first *Critique,* and it is perhaps for this reason that Gadamer finds only one kind of scientific method in the Kantian tradition.[10] Gadamer blames Kant for a fateful dichotomy

10. See Gadamer, *Wahrheit und Methode*, 38. In fact, the neo-Kantians claim that the cultural sciences are not law-oriented or nomothetic in method like the natural sciences, but ideographic or individuating.

between an epistemology that models all objective knowledge on the natural sciences and an aesthetics that is concerned with the mere satisfaction of subjective needs. Instead, we have argued that aesthetic judgment is an aspect of reflective judgment that has its own methodological implications. Whereas Kant's conception of natural science is rigidly mathematical and explanatory in terms of mechanistic causality, reflective judgment provides the basis for both a teleological description of nature and the interpretation of history.

The significance of our attempt to explicate Kant's response to the French Revolution as an instance of reflective interpretation is that we found it necessary to place reflective judgment into relation with determinant judgment. The intersection of these two modes of judgment makes possible a critical methodology for history and the other human sciences. The reflective interpretation of history requires that moral purposes be related to the reflective framework established not only by the teleological ideas examined in chapter 7 concerning culture and the cosmopolitan society, but also by the aesthetic idea of a communal sense discussed in this chapter. It must be possible for reflective judgment to apply reason to the interpretation of contingent historical facts without, however, diluting the validity of the determinant laws of morality. What is required for the interpretation of history is an *intersection* of determinant and reflective judgments, not an *integration* that would dissolve their differences. To keep interpretation critical we must preserve a sense of the difference between the reason that authenticates norms and the reflection that brings them to bear on the actual world. Accordingly, any reflective judgment about political history is merely an indirect appropriation of the moral insights of reason and must also rely on experiential intimations of progress and aesthetic symbols of hope for its orientation. Without such an imaginative orientation to the future it would be difficult to avoid despair about the way the status quo falls short of the demands of reason. Habermas, who is well known for finding Gadamer's hermeneutics inadequately critical because of its reliance on norms already embodied in the tradition, appeals to "an ideal speech situation" for orientation.[11] Such an ideal may be said to rep-

11. See Habermas, "Vorbereitende Bemerkungen zu einer Theorie der kommunikativen Kompetenz," in Jürgen Habermas and Niklas Luhmann, *Theorie der Gesellschaft oder Sozialtechnologie—Was leistet die Systemforschung?* (Frankfurt am Main: Suhrkamp, 1971), 140.

resent a nontranscendent version of Kantian practical reason, but it lacks the reflective specificity and imaginative flexibility that we have found in Kant's views on authentic interpretation and divinatory history.

Because Kant turned to reflective judgment only when the determinant judgments of theoretical and practical reason left him with indeterminacies, determinant judgment seems to set the agenda for reflective judgment. But by viewing the first *Critique* within the frame of reference supplied by the third *Critique,* we also see that the preliminary interpretations of reflective judgment can precede the explanative claims of determinant judgment. Accordingly, reflective interpretation need not be restricted to the human sciences, but can serve to orient the natural sciences. Kant's systematic interpretation of nature, which is based on a regulative use of rational ideas, occurs within a setting delineated by reflection on the life-world. By extending Kant's claim that reflective judgment functions constitutively for questions of taste and regulatively for questions of teleology in nature (see C_3, intro., ix, 34), we may say that reflective interpretation is constitutive for the human sciences and regulative for the natural sciences.

Although all science may be held to be interpretive in some sense, only in the human sciences, where interpretation involves the constant reinterpretation of an already interpreted life-world, do we reach hermeneutical understanding. Natural scientists can normally dismiss the beliefs of the common understanding in their explanations of natural processes, but it is not possible to ignore them in the human sciences, where reflective interpretation is constitutive. No matter how mistaken our beliefs about human action and motivation may be, they must be referred to, not only in the interpretations, but also in the explanations arrived at in the human sciences. The fact that interpreters in the human sciences must always refer back to human self-understanding—both their own and that of their subjects— makes only this kind of interpretation hermeneutical.[12]

The inclusion of the interpreting subject in the hermeneutic circle need not lead to a resubjectivization of hermeneutics. This is because direct discriminatory judgments using aesthetic and teleological orientation contribute to the process of finding our place within the

12. I have defended this position against the attack on hermeneutics by Michel Foucault in my essay "Hermeneutics and the Limits of Consciousness," *Nous* 21 (Spring 1987): 7–18.

overall horizon of the life-world. It is within this horizon that we can then articulate more limited systematic contexts in the way that Kant's teleological ideas can project a variety of purposive systems—organic, social, and cultural. The subject can step back from such contexts and consider them as objectifications to be analyzed and compared. But ultimately the detailed knowledge obtained in the human sciences through such analysis must be related back to the original life-world. In so doing, the goal of hermeneutics should reflect the Kantian ideal of enlarged thought in which we expand our common perspective through imagination and interpretation while maintaining our critical bearings.

Bibliography

Kant's Works

The standard German edition of Kant's complete works is *Kants gesammelte Schriften, herausgegeben von der Preussischen Akademie der Wissenschaften zu Berlin,* 29 vols. (Berlin: Walter de Gruyter, 1902–83). The following English translations have been used or consulted in this volume. Whenever I have revised these translations, I also list the volume and page numbers of the Academy edition.

Anthropology from a Pragmatic Point of View. Trans. Mary J. Gregor. The Hague: Martinus Nijhoff, 1974.
Conflict of the Faculties. Intro. Mary J. Gregor, Trans. M. Gregor and Robert E. Anchor. New York: Abaris Press, 1979.
"Conjectural Beginning of Human History." Trans. Emil Fackenheim. In *Kant on History,* ed. Lewis White Beck, 53–68. Indianapolis: Bobbs-Merrill, 1963.
Critique of Judgment. Trans. J. H. Bernard. New York: Hafner Press, 1974.
Critique of Judgement (consulted only). Trans. J. C. Meredith. Oxford: Clarendon Press, 1964.
Critique of Judgment (consulted only). Trans. Werner Pluhar. Indianapolis: Hackett, 1987.
Critique of Practical Reason. Trans. Lewis White Beck. Indianapolis: Bobbs-Merrill, 1977.
Critique of Pure Reason. Trans. Norman Kemp Smith. New York: St. Martin's Press, 1965.
Dreams of a Spirit-Seer, Illustrated by Dreams of Metaphysics. Trans. Emanuel F. Goerwitz. New York: Macmillan, 1900.
First Introduction to the Critique of Judgment. Trans. James Haden. Indianapolis: Bobbs-Merrill, 1965.
Foundation of the Metaphysics of Morals. Trans. Lewis White Beck. Indianapolis: Bobbs-Merrill, 1959.
"Idea for a Universal History from the Cosmopolitan Point of View." Trans. Lewis White Beck. In *Kant on History,* ed. L. W. Beck, 11–26. Indianapolis: Bobbs-Merrill, 1963.
Lectures on Ethics. Trans. Louis Infield. Indianapolis: Hackett, 1980.

Logic: A Manual for Lectures. Trans. Robert S. Hartman and Wolfgang Schwarz. Indianapolis: Bobbs-Merrill, 1974.

Metaphysical Elements of Justice. Trans. John Ladd. Indianapolis: Bobbs-Merrill, 1965.

Metaphysical Foundations of Natural Science. Trans. James Ellington. Indianapolis: Bobbs-Merrill, 1970.

Metaphysical Principles of Virtue. Trans. James Ellington. Indianapolis: Bobbs-Merrill, 1964.

"On the Failure of All Attempted Philosophical Theodicies." Trans. Michel Despland. In Despland, *Kant on History and Religion,* 283–97. Montreal: McGill-Queen's University Press, 1973.

"On the First Ground of the Distinction of Regions in Space." Trans. John Handyside. In John Handyside and Norman Kemp Smith, eds., *Kant's Inaugural Dissertation and Early Writings on Space.* Chicago: Open Court, 1929.

On the Old Saw: That May Be Right in Theory but It Won't Work in Practice. Trans. E. B. Ashton. Philadelphia: University of Pennsylvania Press, 1974.

"Perpetual Peace." Trans. Lewis White Beck. In *Kant on History,* ed. L. W. Beck, 85–135. Indianapolis: Bobbs-Merrill, 1963.

Prolegomena to Any Future Metaphysics. Trans. G. Carus and L. W. Beck. Indianapolis: Bobbs-Merrill, 1950.

Religion within the Limits of Reason Alone. Trans. T. M. Greene and H. H. Hudson. New York: Harper Torchbooks, 1960.

"What Is Enlightenment?" Trans. Lewis White Beck. In *Kant on History,* ed. L. W. Beck, 3–10. Indianapolis: Library of Liberal Arts, 1963.

"What Is Orientation in Thinking?" Trans. Lewis White Beck. In *Kant's "Critique of Practical Reason" and Other Writings on Moral Philosophy,* ed. L. W. Beck, 293–305. Chicago: University of Chicago Press, 1949.

Secondary Works

Allison, Henry E. *Kant's Transcendental Idealism.* New Haven: Yale University Press, 1983.

Arendt, Hannah. *Lectures on Kant's Political Philosophy.* Chicago: University of Chicago Press, 1982.

Baeumler, Alfred. *Das Irrationalitätsproblem in der Ästhetik und Logik des 18. Jahrhunderts bis zur "Kritik der Urteilskraft."* Darmstadt: Wissenschaftliche Buchgesellschaft, 1974.

Bartuschat, Wolfgang. *Zum systematischen Ort von Kants "Kritik der Urteilskraft."* Frankfurt am Main: Vittorio Klostermann, 1972.

Baumgarten, A. G. *Aesthetica.* Hildesheim: Georg Olms, 1970.

————. *Metaphysica.* Hildesheim: Georg Olms, 1963.

————. *Theoretische Ästhetik.* Hamburg: Felix Meiner Verlag, 1983.

Beck, Lewis White. *A Commentary on Kant's "Critique of Practical Reason."* Chicago: University of Chicago Press, 1966.

————. *Essays on Kant and Hume.* New Haven: Yale University Press, 1978.

Beiner, Ronald. *Political Judgment*. Chicago: University of Chicago Press, 1983.

Bohatec, Josef. *Die Religionsphilosophie Kants in der "Religion innerhalb der Grenzen der bloßen Vernunft."* Hildesheim: Georg Olms Verlagsbuchhandlung, 1966.

Booth, William James. *Interpreting the World: Kant's Philosophy of History and Politics*. Toronto: University of Toronto Press, 1986.

Brandt, Reinhard. *Die Interpretation philosophischer Werke*. Stuttgart-Bad Cannstatt: Frommann-Holzboog, 1984.

Brittan, Gordon G. *Kant's Theory of Science*. Princeton: Princeton University Press, 1978.

Carnois, Bernard. *The Coherence of Kant's Doctrine of Freedom*. Trans. David Booth. Chicago: University of Chicago Press, 1987.

Casey, Edward S. *Imagining: A Phenomenological Study*. Bloomington: Indiana University Press, 1976.

Cassirer, Ernst. *Kant's Life and Thought*. Trans. James Haden. New Haven: Yale University Press, 1981.

_____. *The Philosophy of the Enlightenment*. Trans. F. C. A. Koelln and J. P. Pettegrove. Princeton: Princeton University Press, 1951.

Coleman, Francis X. J. *The Harmony of Reason: A Study in Kant's Aesthetics*. Pittsburgh: University of Pittsburgh Press, 1974.

Crawford, Donald W. *Kant's Aesthetic Theory*. Madison: The University of Wisconsin Press, 1974.

Deleuze, Gilles. *Kant's Critical Philosophy*. Minneapolis: University of Minnesota Press, 1984.

Despland, Michel. *Kant on History and Religion*. Montreal and London: McGill-Queen's University Press, 1973.

Dilthey, Wilhelm. *Gesammelte Schriften*. 19 vols. Göttingen: Vandenhoeck & Ruprecht, 1914–1982.

Düsing, Klaus. *Die Teleologie in Kants Weltbegriff*. Kantstudien Ergänzungshefte, 96. Bonn: H. Bouvier u. Co. Verlag, 1968.

Engell, James. *The Creative Imagination: Enlightenment to Romanticism*. Cambridge: Harvard University Press, 1981.

Ewing, A. C. *A Short Commentary on Kant's "Critique of Pure Reason."* Chicago: University of Chicago Press, 1967.

Frieden, Ken. *Genius and Monologue*. Ithaca: Cornell University Press, 1985.

Gadamer, Hans-Georg. *Wahrheit und Methode*. 2d ed. Tübingen: J. C. B. Mohr, 1965.

Galston, William A. *Kant and the Problem of History*. Chicago: University of Chicago Press, 1975.

Goldmann, Lucien. *Immanuel Kant*. London: NLB, 1971.

Gram, Moltke S., ed. *Interpreting Kant*. Iowa City: University of Iowa Press, 1982.

Gulyga, Arsenji. *Immanuel Kant*. German translation by Sigrun Bielfeldt. Frankfurt am Main: Insel Verlag, 1981.

Guyer, Paul. *Kant and the Claims of Taste*. Cambridge: Harvard University Press, 1979.

Heidegger, Martin. *Phänomenologische Interpretation von Kants "Kritik der reinen Vernunft." Gesamtausgabe*. Abteilung: Vorlesungen 1923–1944. Vol. 25. Frankfurt am Main: Vittorio Klostermann, 1977.

———. *Kant and the Problem of Metaphysics*. Bloomington: Indiana University Press, 1962.

Heintel, Peter. *Die Bedeutung der Kritik der ästhetischen Urteilskraft für die transzendentale Systematik*. Kantstudien Ergänzungshefte, 99. Bonn: H. Bouvier u. Co. Verlag, 1970.

Hirsch, E. D. *Validity in Interpretation*. New Haven: Yale University Press, 1967.

Howard, Dick. *From Marx to Kant*. Albany: State University of New York Press, 1985.

Husserl, Edmund. *Cartesian Meditations*. The Hague: Martinus Nijhoff, 1960.

Hutchings, Patrick. *Kant on Absolute Value*. Detroit: Wayne State University Press, 1972.

Kaulbach, Friedrich. *Ästhetische Welterkenntnis bei Kant*. Würzburg: Königshausen und Neumann, 1984.

Kemal, Salim. *Kant and Fine Art*. Oxford: Clarendon Press, 1986.

Krämling, Gerhard. *Die systembildende Rolle von Ästhetik und Kulturphilosophie bei Kant*. Freiburg/Munich: Verlag Karl Alber, 1985.

Kroner, Richard. *Kant's Weltanschauung*. Trans. John E. Smith. Chicago: University of Chicago Press, 1956.

Krüger, Gerhard. *Philosophie und Moral in der Kantischen Kritik*. Tübingen: J. C. B. Mohr (Paul Siebeck), 1931.

Kuehn, Manfred. *Scottish Common Sense in Germany, 1768–1800*. Montreal: McGill-Queen's University Press, 1987.

Kulenkampff, J., ed. *Materialen zu Kants "Kritik der Urteilskraft."* Frankfurt am Main: Suhrkamp, 1974.

Kuypers, K. *Kants Kunsttheorie und die Einheit der "Kritik der Urteilskraft." Verhandelingen der Koninklijke Nederlandse Akademie van Wetenschappen, AFD. Letterkunde, Nieuwe Reeks, Deel 77, No. 3*. Amsterdam and London: North Holland Publishing Company, 1972.

Leibniz, Gottfried Wilhelm von. *New Essays on Human Understanding*. Trans. and eds. Peter Remnant and Jonathan Bennett. Cambridge: Cambridge University Press, 1982.

Löw, Reinhard. *Philosophie des Lebendigen*. Frankfurt am Main: Suhrkamp, 1980.

Lyotard, Jean-François. *The Postmodern Condition: A Report on Knowledge*. Minneapolis: University of Minnesota Press, 1984.

Lyotard, Jean-François, and Jean-Loup Thebaud. *Just Gaming*. Trans. Wlad Godzick. Minneapolis: University of Minnesota Press, 1985.

Makkreel, Rudolf A. *Dilthey, Philosopher of the Human Studies*. Princeton: Princeton University Press, 1975.

McCloskey, Mary A. *Kant's Aesthetic.* London: Macmillan, 1987.

Merleau-Ponty, Maurice. *The Phenomenology of Perception.* Trans. Colin Smith. London: Routledge and Kegan Paul, 1962.

Mertens, Helga. *Kommentar zur ersten Einleitung in Kants "Kritik der Urteilskraft."* Munich: Johannes Berchmans Verlag, 1975.

Mörchen, Hermann. *Die Einbildungskraft bei Kant.* Tübingen: Max Niemeyer Verlag, 1970.

Mohanty, J. N., and Robert W. Shahan, eds. *Essays on Kant's "Critique of Pure Reason."* Norman: University of Oklahoma Press, 1982.

Nagel, Gordon. *The Structure of Experience: Kant's System of Principles.* Chicago: University of Chicago Press, 1983.

Paton, H. J. *The Categorical Imperative.* London: Hutchinson & Co., 1947.

———. *Kant's Metaphysic of Experience.* London: George Allen & Unwin, 1965.

Pippin, Robert B. *Kant's Theory of Form.* New Haven: Yale University Press, 1982.

Pitte, Frederick van de. *Kant as Philosophical Anthropologist.* The Hague: Martinus Nijhoff, 1971.

Prauss, Gerold. *Erscheinung bei Kant. Ein Problem der "Kritik der reinen Vernunft."* Berlin: Walter de Gruyter & Co., 1971.

Ricoeur, Paul. *Freud and Philosophy: An Essay on Interpretation.* New Haven: Yale University Press, 1970.

———. *Interpretation Theory: Discourse and the Surplus of Meaning.* Fort Worth: Texas Christian University Press, 1976.

Riedel, Manfred. *Urteilskraft und Vernunft: Kants ursprüngliche Fragestellung.* Frankfurt am Main: Suhrkamp, 1989.

Riley, Patrick. *Kant's Political Philosophy.* Totawa, N.J.: Rowman and Littlefield, 1983.

Rogerson, Kenneth F. *Kant's Aesthetics: The Roles of Form and Expression.* Lanham, Md.: University Press of America, 1986.

Rosen, Stanley. *Hermeneutics as Politics.* New York: Oxford University Press, 1987.

Sallis, John. *The Gathering of Reason.* Athens: Ohio University Press, 1980.

———. *Spacings—of Reason and Imagination in Texts of Kant, Fichte, Hegel.* Chicago: University of Chicago Press, 1987.

Sartre, Jean-Paul. *The Psychology of Imagination.* New York: Citadel Press, 1961.

Satura, Vladimir. *Kants Erkenntnispsychologie.* Kantstudien Ergänzungshefte, 101. Bonn: H. Bouvier u. Co. Verlag Hermann Grundmann, 1971.

Schaper, Eva. *Studies in Kant's Aesthetics.* Edinburgh: Edinburgh University Press, 1979.

Schiller, Friedrich. *On the Aesthetic Education of Man.* Trans. E. M. Wilkinson and L. A. Willoughby. Oxford: The Clarendon Press, 1967.

Schlapp, Otto. *Kants Lehre vom Genie und die Entstehung der "Kritik der Urteilskraft."* Göttingen: Vandenhoeck & Ruprecht, 1901.

Schweizer, Hans Rudolf. *Asthetik als Philosophie der sinnlichen Erkenntnis.* Basel/Stuttgart: Schwabe & Co., 1973.

Scruton, Robert. *Art and Imagination: A Study in the Philosophy of Mind.* London: Routledge & Kegan Paul, 1974.

Seebohm, Thomas M., and Joseph J. Kockelmans, eds. *Kant and Phenomenology.* Washington, D.C.: Center for Advanced Research in Phenomenology & University Press of America, 1984.

Shell, Susan Meld. *The Rights of Reason: A Study of Kant's Philosophy and Politics.* Toronto: University of Toronto Press, 1980.

Smith, Norman Kemp. *A Commentary to Kant's "Critique of Pure Reason."* New York: Humanities Press, 1962.

Strawson, P. F. *The Bounds of Sense: An Essay on Kant's "Critique of Pure Reason."* London: Methuen & Co. Ltd. 1966.

Stuckenberg, J. H. W. *The Life of Immanuel Kant.* London: Macmillan and Co., 1882.

Tetens, Johann Nicolas. *Philosophische Versuche über die menschliche Natur und ihre Entwicklung.* Vol. 1 (1777). In *Neudrücke der Kant-Gesellschaft,* vol. 4. Berlin: Verlag von Reuther and Reichard, 1913.

Trebels, Andreas Heinrich. *Einbildungskraft und Spiel: Untersuchungen zur Kantischen Ästhetik.* Kantstudien Ergänzungshefte, 93. Bonn: H. Bouvier u. Co. Verlag, 1967.

Uehling, Theodore. *The Notion of Form in Kant's Critique of Aesthetic Judgment.* The Hague: Mouton, 1971.

Vico, Giambattista. *The New Science.* Ithaca: Cornell University Press, 1984.

Ward, Keith. *The Development of Kant's View of Ethics.* Oxford: Basil Blackwell, 1972.

Wolff, Christian. *Vernünftige Gedanken von Gott, der Welt und der Seele des Menschen.* Hildesheim: George Olms, 1983.

Wolff, Robert Paul. *Kant's Theory of Mental Activity.* Cambridge: Harvard University Press, 1963.

Wood, Allen W. *Kant's Moral Religion.* Ithaca and London: Cornell University Press, 1970.

Yovel, Yirmiahu. *Kant and the Philosophy of History.* Princeton: Princeton University Press, 1980.

Articles

Abrams, M. H. "Kant and the Theology of Art." *Notre Dame English Journal* 13 (1981): 75–106.

Butts, Robert E. "Kant's Schemata as Semantical Rules." In *Kant Studies Today,* ed. Lewis White Beck, 290–300. La Salle, Illinois: Open Court, 1969.

Cassirer, Ernst. "Geist und Leben in der Philosophie der Gegenwart." *Die Neue Rundschau* 41 (1930): 244–64.

Crawford, Donald W. "The Place of the Sublime in Kant's Aesthetic Theory." In *The Philosophy of Immanuel Kant,* ed. Richard Kennington, 161–83. Washington, D.C.: Catholic University of America Press, 1985.

de Man, Paul. "Phenomenality and Materiality in Kant." In *Hermeneutics:*

Questions and Prospects, eds. Gary Shapiro and Alan Sica, 121–44. Amherst: University of Massachusetts Press, 1984.

Derrida, Jacques. "Mochlos ou le conflit des facultés." *Philosophie* 2 (1984): 21–53.

Dostal, Robert J. "Kantian Aesthetics and the Literary Criticism of E. D. Hirsch." *Journal of Aesthetics and Art Criticism* 38, no. 3 (Spring 1980): 299–305.

Fackenheim, Emil. "Kant's Concept of History." *Kant-Studien* 48 (1956/57): 381–98.

Fisher, John, and Maitland, Jeffrey. "The Subjectivist Turn in Aesthetics: A Critical Analysis of Kant's Theory of Appreciation." *Review of Metaphysics* 27 (1974): 726–51.

Genova, Anthony C. "Kant's Complex Problem of Reflective Judgment." *Review of Metaphysics* 23 (1970): 452–80.

Goethe, Johann Wolfgang von. "Einwirkung der neuern Philosophie." In *Goethes Werke.* Part 2, vol. 11, 47–53. Weimar: Hermann Böhlan, 1893.

Gregor, Mary J. "Aesthetic Form and Sensory Content." In *The Philosophy of Immanuel Kant,* ed. Richard Kennington, 185–99. Washington, D.C.: The Catholic University of America Press, 1985.

———. "Baumgarten's *Aesthetica.*" *Review of Metaphysics* 37, no. 2 (December 1983): 357–85.

Hamacher, Werner. "'Das Versprechen der Auslegung': Überlegungen zum hermeneutischen Imperative bei Kant und Nietzsche." In *Spiegel und Gleichnis,* eds. N. Bolz and W. Hübener, 252–73. Würzburg, Königshausen & Neumann, 1983.

Henrich, Dieter. "Über die Einheit der Subjektivität." *Philosophische Rundschau* 3 (1955): 44–73.

Johnson, Mark L. "Kant's Unified Theory of Beauty." *Journal of Aesthetics and Art Criticism* 38 (1978): 167–78.

Kuhns, Richard. "That Kant Did Not Complete His Argument Concerning the Relation of Art to Morality and How It Might Be Completed." *Idealistic Studies* 5 (1975): 190–206.

Lazaroff, Allan. "The Kantian Sublime: Aesthetic Judgment and Religious Feeling." *Kant-Studien* 71 (1980): 202–20.

Makkreel, Rudolf A. "The Feeling of Life: Some Kantian Sources of Life-Philosophy." *Dilthey-Jahrbuch für Philosophie und Geschichte der Geisteswissenschaften* 3 (1985): 83–104.

———. "Hermeneutics and the Limits of Consciousness." *Nous* 21 (Spring 1987): 7–18.

———. "Imagination and Temporality in Kant's Theory of the Sublime." *Journal of Aesthetics and Art Criticism* 42 (Spring 1984): 303–15.

———. "The Role of Synthesis in Kant's *Critique of Judgment.*" In *Proceedings of the Sixth International Kant Congress.* Forthcoming.

———. "Tradition and Orientation in Hermeneutics." *Research in Phenomenology* 26 (1986): 73–85.

Meerbote, Ralf. "Reflections on Beauty." In *Essays in Kant's Aesthetics,* eds. Ted Cohen and Paul Guyer, 55–86. Chicago: University of Chicago Press, 1982.

Nahm, Milton C. "'Sublimity' and the 'Moral Law' in Kant's Philosophy."
    Kant-Studien 48 (1956–57): 502–24.
Neville, Michael R. "Kant on Beauty as the Symbol of Morality." *Philosophy
    Research Archives* 1 (1975), no. 1053.
Sherover, Charles. "Two Kinds of Transcendental Objectivity: Their Differ-
    entiation." In *Essays on Kant's "Critique of Pure Reason,"* eds. J. N. Mohanty
    and Robert W. Shahan, 251–78. Norman: University of Oklahoma Press,
    1982.
Tarbet, David W. "The Fabric of Metaphor in Kant's *Critique of Pure Reason*."
    Journal of the History of Philosophy 6 (July 1968): 257–70.
Vollrath, Ernst. "Kants *Kritik der Urteilskraft* als Grundlegung einer Theorie
    des Politischen." In *Akten des 4. Internationalen Kant-Kongresses,* ed. G.
    Funke, 692–705. Berlin: Walter de Gruyter, 1974.
Williams, Forrest. "Philosophical Anthropology and the Critique of Aesthet-
    ic Judgment." *Kant-Studien* 46 (1954–55): 172–88.
J. Michael Young. "Kant's View of Imagination." *Kant-Studien* 79 (1988):
    140–64.
Zeldin, Barbara. "Pleasure, Life and Mother-Wit." In *Freedom and the Critical
    Undertaking: Essays in Kant's Later Critique,* 116–39. Ann Arbor: Univer-
    sity Microfilms International, 1980.
Zimmerman, Robert L. "Kant: The Aesthetic Judgment." In *Kant: A Collec-
    tion of Critical Essays,* ed. Robert Paul Wolff, 385–406. Garden City, N.Y.:
    Doubleday & Co., 1967.

Index